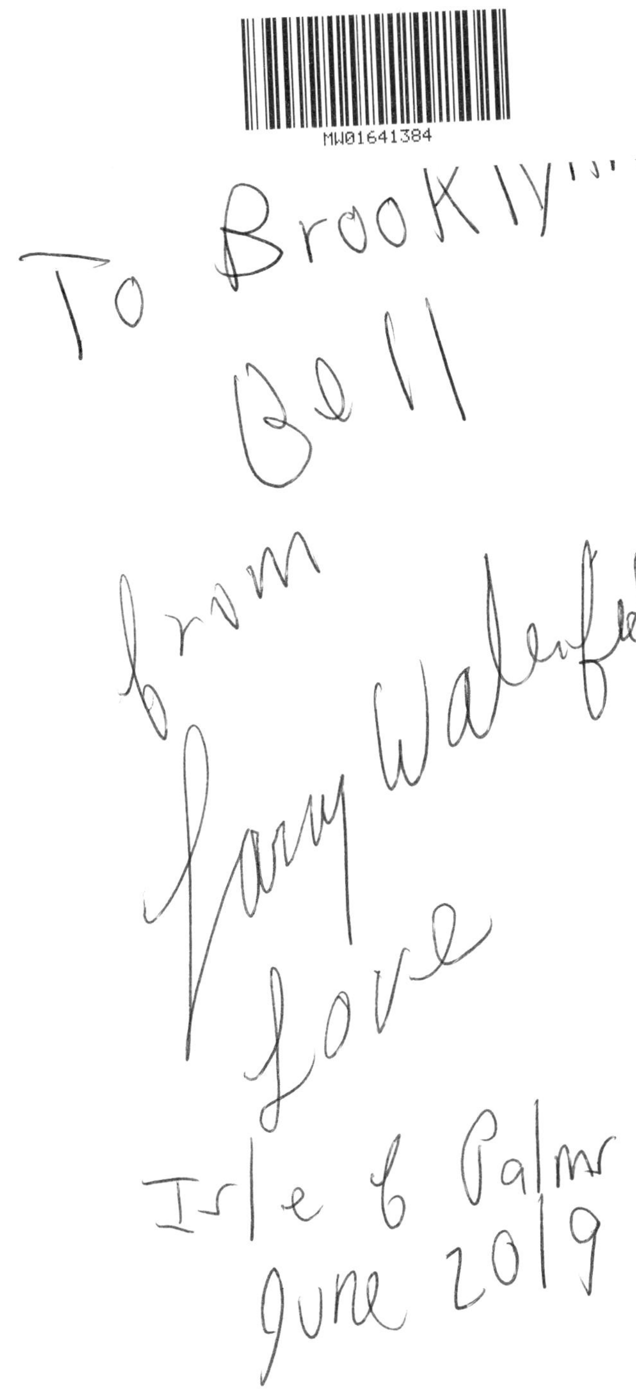
MW01641384
To Brooklyn
Bell
from
Larry Wakefield
Love
Isle of Palms
June 2019

Larry W. Waterfield is a journalist, author, and illustrator in Washington, D.C. He has covered news and events around the world. He ran a magazine news bureau in Washington for a number of years. His articles have appeared in magazines and newspapers in the U.S., Britain, Europe, and Latin America. He has worked as an editor, columnist, videographer, photographer, book author. He is also an illustrator producing poster and print art on history, architecture, travel, and other topics. He studied European History at the University of Missouri and received a Journalism degree from the University of Missouri School of Journalism, where he also did graduate work. He is married and lives in Fairfax, Virginia.

Larry W. Waterfield

Metropolis at War: London

Biography of a Great City in Crisis

Austin Macauley Publishers™
London • Cambridge • New York • Sharjah

Ordering Information:
Quantity sales: special discounts are available on quantity purchases by corporations, associations, and others. For details, contact the publisher at the address below.

Publisher's Cataloging-in-Publication data
Waterfield, Larry W.
Metropolis at War: London

ISBN 9781641821452 (Paperback)
ISBN 9781641821445 (Hardback)
ISBN 9781641821438 (E-Book)

The main category of the book: History / Europe / Great Britain / 20th Century

www.austinmacauley.com/us

First Published (2019)
Austin Macauley Publishers LLC
40 Wall Street, 28th Floor
New York, NY 10005
USA

mail-usa@austinmacauley.com
+1 (646) 5125767

Outline of the Contents

AN INTRODUCTION

1. Imperial Capital: London as head of an Empire where the sun never sets.
   a. Biggest City in the World
   b. Capital of a Nation and an Empire
   c. A threatened metropolis.

2. War on Land, at Sea, in the Air
   a. Outbreak of WWII
   b. Hitler Triumphant
   c. London fights back

3. Coalition Government and Total War
   a. Socialists and Conservatives share power.
   b. Total Mobilization: 17 million in military and war work. Women at war.
   c. Preparing for the worst. Plan to move the Government from London—The Black Move.

4. Blitz over Britain and London.
   a. Bombs fall day and night.
   b. The defenses and evacuation.
   c. London resists. Deep shelters.
   d. Life in the Subways and shelters.

5. Threat of Invasion, Starvation, Defeat.
   a. Desperate plans to defend the city, nation.
   b. Poison gas. Chemical warfare. Suicide squads.
   c. The evil prospect of defeat.
   d. Churchill's war using words.
   e. Hitler's ugly plans for occupation of Britain: the Black Book of arrest and death. Fate of the Jews.

f. Elaborate British plans to invade neutral Ireland in the fight against Hitler.

6. A World at War—fighting on 3 continents.
   a. The Empire strikes back.
   b. British fleets and forces around the world, from North Africa to Palestine to India and Malaya—Singapore.
   a. Battle of the Atlantic and beyond. Merchant Navy loses 2,400 ships, 32,000 sailors in order to supply necessities.

7. Death from Space—A Second Blitz—the world's first rocket attack on a great city. Thousands hit London.
   a. Countering the missiles.
   b. World's first jet plane sees action—against rockets.

8. Secret Wars: Spies, Saboteurs, Commandos
   a. The intelligence war. 'Ultra' success.
   b. Propaganda War: London Calling.
   c. Germany Calling.
   d. The War of Deception.

   e. Bush House—BBC speaks to the world in dozens of languages.
   f. The secret messages.
   g. The great and deadly Soviet spy ring aimed at London.
   h. World's most successful spy? Klaus Fuchs.
   i. Britain's Secret 'Terror Army'
   j. Spies, good, bad, terrible.

9. Disaster in Asia: London reacts.
   a. 'Worst Defeat' in Singapore. Worst intelligence failure ever.
   b. Crisis in India.
   c. Britain vs. the Empire of Japan. Saving India.

10. London: City of Exiles.
    a. Eleven governments in Exile.

    b. The Exiles take the fight Home.
    c. The Poles expose the Holocaust via BBC.

11. Preparing for the Birth of Israel:
    a. Israel's future leaders in London.
    b. The thankless task of running Palestine.
    c. Deadly birth pangs of a new nation.

12. The People's War.
    a. On the Home front: How the City survives.
    b. 'The end of the good life.' Rationing. Fate of famous hotels, restaurants.
    c. Keeping up Morale: Movies, music, theatre and more. 'Hollywood on the Thames.'

13. War of the Words—London's Raucous Wartime Press.
14. Americans—'over fed, over-sexed, over here'.
15. What did You Do in the War? Famous writers, filmmakers, scientists, thinkers, economists, spies, actors were in war-time London. What were they doing?

16. Tomorrow, Just You Wait and See.
    a. Hope on the Horizon.
    b. A string of Victories.
    c. Beginning of the End.

17. Peace—and Revolution
    a. Defeat of Hitler, Japan. A Brief Euphoria.
    b. Churchill voted out.
    c. Labour—Socialist victory leads to nationalization of industry, a national health system, 'socialized medicine', an end of Empire in India, elsewhere. Birth of the Welfare State.
    d. London rebuilt, revived, finds a new role in the world.

"Its greatest moment may have been its last great moment."

Appendix

British forces around the world commanded from London, domestic war workers, civil defense, Home Guard, etc.

Wartime losses in the city: dead, wounded, evacuations, destroyed buildings and houses. The city then and now.

Table of Contents

Chapter 1
Metropolis in Mortal Danger

In 1939, on the eve of World War II, London was the largest city in the world. It was also about to become the most threatened city. It would be the first world metropolis to come under sustained attack by modern warfare, first by aerial bombardment, then by rockets and missiles.

London, capital of Britain and Northern Ireland, and of a vast worldwide Empire, was the biggest target of all, both in terms of people, area, and geopolitical importance.

It is hard to imagine now the size and scope of that Empire controlled from London. At the time of the war, it encompassed 532 million people on every continent and spread over more than 10 million square miles. Some parts were ruled directly from London: Palestine, Singapore, Hong Kong, African colonies; various dependencies, protectorates, and mandates. Egypt and even Iraq were under British protection and control. Other states, Dominions of the Commonwealth, such as Canada, Australia, South Africa, governed themselves but followed London's lead and foreign policy. The biggest slice of all, India, with 390 million people, was ruled by the British Raj and a viceroy sent from London.

Some 8.5 million people lived in London itself, spread over 600 square miles. Within 25 miles of the center, Charing Cross, lived more than 10 million. Within the commuting area, called the Home Counties—60 to 90 minutes by rail—lived perhaps another 2–3 million people.

In land area, London was bigger than New York and Berlin combined. The dense 'inner London' of 117 square miles was home to 4.5 million people.

London was a gritty northern city, known for its smog, fog and mists; its confusing jumble of streets with changing names.

It had a certain grandeur, exemplified by massive buildings interspersed with charming Christopher Wren churches; crescent streets, gleaming white terraces, and palaces guarded by tall men in bearskin hats.

The vast East End was poor and cockney; the West End, ritzy and purveyor of the good life. In the middle was the City, the financial district, with its buttoned-down bankers in bowlers and sporting tightly-rolled brollies—umbrellas.

There were many Londons and everyone knew it in a different way. Low and nasty, haughty and aloof. In *Bleak House*, Charles Dickens saw 'Much mud in the streets… Fog everywhere… And hard by Temple Bar, in Lincoln's Inn Hall, at the very heart of the fog, sits the Lord High Chancellor in his High Court of Chancery.'

The poet A. E. Housman saw a heartless city through the eyes of a country lad, where the people are:

'Too unhappy to be kind.
Undone with misery, all they can
Is to hate their fellow man;'

To the romantic Wordsworth, it was a magical city where:

'Ships, towers, domes, theaters, and temples lie
Open unto the fields, and to the sky;
All bright and glittering in smokeless air.'

London was black cabs and nannies pushing prams. It was the private clubs of 'The Establishment', the movers, and shakers. It was the center of live theater; it was the media center, with huge-circulation newspapers lining Fleet Street. It was a moviemaking center, with 11 active film studios. It was the home of a generally competent and professional Civil Service. Parliament and the Prime Minister made it the political center.

It was not an ethnic city. It was peopled with Englishmen, with communities of Welsh, Scots, and the Irish. That was about to change as thousands of folks from conquered Europe flowed in; Poles, French, Czechs, Dutch, even some Germans and Austrians.

The metropolis sometimes seemed undecipherable. In 1935, writer Phyllis Pearsall got lost in London's street maze. She got mad, got busy and worked with a cartographer, and over the next year created *London A-Z*, a street atlas in wide use today. She eventually identified 70,000 streets, roads, avenues, squares and alleyways.

If New York was all hustle among skyscrapers, and Paris the elegant city of grand boulevards, then London emanated strength and power.

'London is a man's town, there's power in the air' wrote the poet Henry Van Dyke.

London was busy and at peace in September, 1939 when war broke out with Germany, which launched an all-out attack on Poland, by order of Adolph Hitler, with a coordinated assault on land, sea and by air. Blitz war was the tactic; strikes with lightning speed using tanks, mechanized divisions, dive bombers, and heavy bombers. Paratroopers dropped behind enemy lines. Civilians fleeing the war were attacked to create chaos, and block roads and access to the front.

Warsaw, the capital, a city of 1.4 million, was heavily bombed and large sections were hit, destroyed, and set on fire. Poland fell quickly after a courageous but futile fight. Then the bombardment stopped. A period of calm ensued between Germany and the Western Allies, Britain and France.

Then, in 1940, Germany attacked westward, sweeping over Belgium, the Netherlands, Luxembourg and into France. British and French forces battled against the new Blitz invasion. They were quickly pushed back to the English Channel, and squeezed into a pocket. It was a military disaster.

Hundreds of ships, boats, and vessels of every description left British ports to rescue the troops trapped on the beach at Dunkirk, France. In the 'miracle of the little ships' some 340,000 British and French troops were saved and brought to Britain. Still, thousands of tanks, trucks, and guns were lost, along with tens of thousands of soldiers.

France fell quickly after that and sued for peace. The country was partitioned, with the northern part under German occupation, the southern part under a government willing to cooperate with Hitler, and with a capital at the spa town of Vichy. Old Marshall Phillipe Pètain, veteran soldier, was installed as president of Vichy France.

Now Hitler, the Nazis, and their allies in Fascist Italy controlled most of Europe; from Poland to the English Channel, from North African colonies to the Arctic Circle in Norway.

German and Italian forces were threatening to conquer the states of North Africa, Egypt, the Suez Canal, and the Middle East. Russia was neutral, as was the United States. Now Britain stood alone on its island. A new leader, Winston Churchill, vowed to keep fighting even though Hitler indicated a peace deal could be struck. Britain could perhaps save itself and even keep its empire. Britain would end any opposition to Hitler in return for...survival. Any deviation or hesitation would bring renewed threat of invasion. Hitler might change his mind on a whim.

Churchill and his war cabinet rejected the overtures of peace. It would have amounted to virtual surrender. At the same time, Churchill knew Hitler had to eliminate Britain. He said: "Hitler knows he must defeat us in our island or lose the war." Churchill had opposed moves to 'appease' Hitler; he had contempt for the Austrian corporal who now ruled Greater Germany. Churchill was a soldier, a fighter by training, nature, and history. When it became clear Churchill would not knuckle under, Hitler ordered the German military and the SS, the Nazi party army, to draw up plans for the invasion and occupation of Britain.

At this point, the smart money would not have bet on Britain surviving. U.S. ambassador to London, Joseph P. Kennedy, father of future President Jack Kennedy, was pessimistic to the point where British officials considered him 'defeatist'. He had supported accommodation with Hitler—appeasement. When the bombs fell, he got out of London.

Soon after that, President Franklin Roosevelt replaced him. Marshal Pètain, as leader of Vichy France and subject to the whims of Hitler, said, "England will have her neck wrung like a chicken."

Churchill replied, "Some chicken!"

There was unity, but not entirely. Just minutes after Churchill spoke to the House of Commons about 'blood, toil, tears and sweat', one long-time member, James Maxton from 'red' Glasgow, and a biographer of Lenin, attacked the failures he said led to war and wholesale slaughter.

He said, "Churchill offered no thought now to peace," and added, "We believe that the overwhelming mass of people of this world, Germany included, are against the slaughter method of life."

His words prompted derision in the House, which went on to vote in favor of the new war coalition government, 381 to 0. Lloyd George, former Liberal Prime Minister and the senior member of the House, was more representative of the mood. He said, "Churchill faced the greatest jeopardy that has ever confronted a prime minister. Friends of freedom wish you God speed."

At this point, Britain, a nation of nearly 50 million people, was in a poor position to defend itself against Germany, Italy and the conquered nations—home to 270 million people and vast military, scientific and industrial resources.

The army had just barely avoided capture by escaping from the beaches of France. That was hardly a victory, only avoidance of total disaster. Britain had a small professional army, and big and powerful navy ships; that was its strongest defensive asset.

But there were many vulnerabilities. London—the vast heart of the nation, home of the government and Royal Family, along with the centers of finance, media, communications, film and broadcasting, and culture—was just 100 miles from the Continent, and only 40 miles from the open sea. More than a million people commuted in and out of Central London every day. Millions more moved by subway, the London Underground. Pulverize London and the whole country might as well grind to a halt.

London was a vital port; a place of manufacturing and distribution. Its East End Docklands were linked to the world. It was the hub of the nation's rail system. Its 11 major train stations were run by the 4 huge private railroad companies that covered the entire country. These companies operated passenger and freight trains, electric commuter trains, boat trains, ferries, ships, port facilities, delivery trucks, hotels, restaurants, and resorts. Collectively, the Big Four employed nearly 800,000 workers and served every town and village. They carried the goods, the mail, the food, and fuel for a nation. The largest company, the London, Midland and Scottish Railway was the world's largest private transportation company. The others: Great Western, Southern, and London and Northeastern were nearly as large as the LMS. The country ran on the rails. To conquer London and defeat Britain, the railways and the great London hub would have to be pounded into twisted steel and ruination.

The daily rhythm of the metropolis didn't just include railways. London Transport's famous subways and double-decker buses carried five million people every day. Disrupt this internal system, and work and life break down. Another great vulnerability, perhaps the most serious, was food. Britain produced food for only half its people. Thus, every day the country had to import food to feed nearly 25 million people—three New York cities. Some products were overwhelmingly dependent on imports: 50% of meat, 80% of fresh fruit. Disrupt these imports, impose a blockade, and sink the supply ships, and in a few months starvation would be a real threat. Food would have to be severely rationed, with its dire effect on morale and fighting ability. Malnutrition would be inevitable, and starvation likely. Some foods—citrus, tropical fruits—would disappear completely. Domestic meat would largely disappear—animals consume too much vital grain.

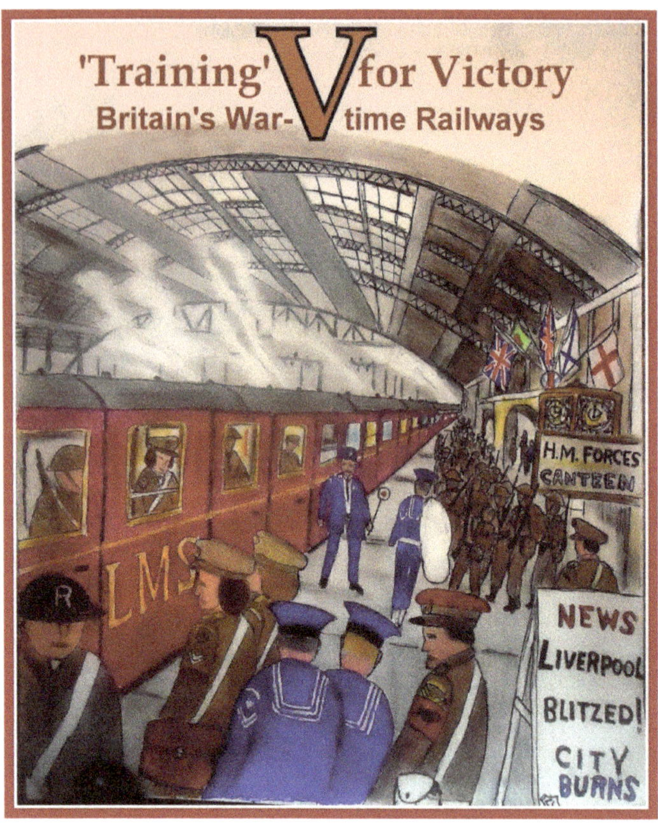

Invasion—the Plan

The regular German armed forces, the Wehrmacht (army), Luftwaffe (air force) and Navy (Kriegsmarine), plus the forces tied to the Nazi party (SS, Security Service, Gestapo) began laying plans to invade, conquer, and occupy Britain.

A big part of the plan centered on London. The great city would not be attacked directly from the ground. It would be encircled, enveloped, cut off, and then starved out.

In general, the plan would proceed this way:

- Destroy the Air Force, RAF, to gain air control.
- Destroy the new radar stations that gave advanced warning.
- Attack and destroy airfields, airplane factories, rail hubs, and war-making facilities.
- Keep the powerful Royal Navy bottled up or at bay.
- Blockade the sea lanes with submarines and heavy warships.
- Sink any and all ships carrying food, fuel, supplies, weapons, and troops. (This meant sink all ships.)
- Invade the south coast with elite forces along a hundred-mile front. Use Blitz warfare, heavy armor, paratroopers dropped in the rear areas, plus elite special forces.
- Seize a major port and establish a beachhead.
- Rapidly build up forces and strike inland to encircle London and cut the country in two.
- Crush all resistance, brutally suppress any opposition, local, civilian, militia (Home Guard.)
- After the country is conquered and pacified, including London, complete any mopping-up operations. Brutally suppress any insurgency or local resistance.
- Establish an occupation government. Arrest and possibly eliminate the leaders, public figures, anti-German citizens, exiles and others in the Black Book, a list of 2800 names compiled by the SS. (Enemy #1: Winston S. Churchill).
- Eliminate all 'anti-German' organizations, including the Boy Scouts, Freemasons, Labor Unions, Communist Party.
- Eliminate Britain's 300,000 Jews, most of whom lived in London.
- Appoint national and regional overlords to rule the country. Perhaps appoint a puppet British leader, if one could be found. Set up the whole occupation infrastructure of police, secret police, security, and military to keep total control.

- Take control of industry, science and technology, military bases and equipment and use them to further the goals of the Hitler regime.
- Organize working-age men into forced labor battalions and ship many of them to Continental Europe.

The invasion plan was code-named *Sealion.* There was nothing in the plan about the terror-bombing of London. That would arise as events unfolded in ways no one anticipated.

Although it was later in the war that Nazi propaganda minister Joseph Goebbels would give his infamous 'Total War' speech at the Berlin Sportpalast, Hitler's invasion plan hinted at something close to total war. Any civilians in the way of the juggernaut would be run over.

The German war planners perfected their plan in precise detail. Their invasion material even included post cards and tourist photos of British beach resorts so invaders would recognize the look of the places.

One big source of intelligence was a travel book, *Karl Baedeker's 1937 Guide to Great Britain,* by the German publisher. This tome was a detailed description of every city, town, village, port, industry, rail hub, and bridge. It even described the contents of castles, cathedrals, and countless buildings of every description, including government offices. It included details of naval bases, dry docks, barracks, military installations, headquarters, military schools, and training and testing grounds. Every rail tunnel and its length was listed, along with airfields, power plants, and oil docks.

The Germans landed some agents on the beaches, but they were quickly caught. Spying efforts largely failed. Unknown to the Germans, the British had broken their communication code.

The invaders would be divided into two army groups, A and C. The invasion force would consist of infantry and mountain troops, paratroopers, followed by tank and mechanized divisions and special forces—'Blitz' war.

In all, as many as 40 divisions would be involved. This was later pared back to 25 divisions to be landed in 3 waves. They would land on the south coast opposite France, from the Thames Estuary to the big port and naval base of Portsmouth and beyond. Much of that coast is bordered by cliffs and hills. A key landing target were the Romney Marshes almost straight south of London. These drained marshes were flat ground. (The British took the precaution to flood the marshes.)

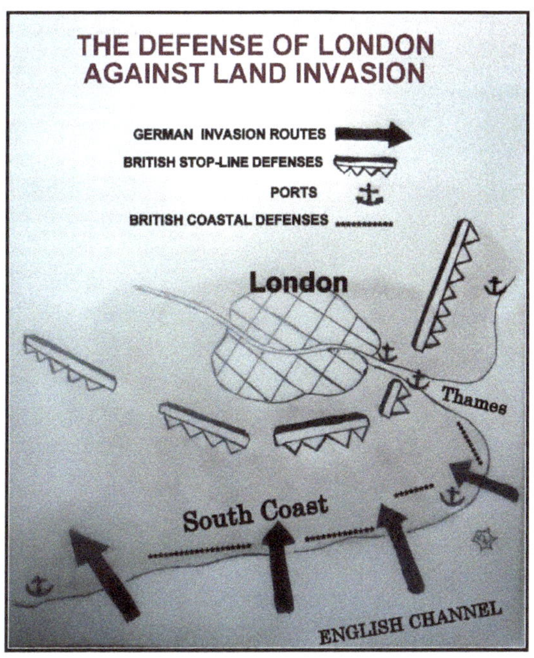

The invasion troops would embark in French and Belgian ports close to England, including Antwerp, Ostend, Calais, Dieppe, Cherbourg, and Le Havre. Staging areas for troops, tanks, and equipment stretched miles inland. One landing would take place near the big resort of Brighton, at or near the town of Worthing. The first wave of troops would secure the beaches, breakthrough what British planners called the coastal crust of mines, barbed wire, tank barriers, and gun emplacements.

The second wave would consist of the heavy divisions, tanks and armor (Panzers) and mechanized troops, with Grenadier assault infantry. This wave would number 3 divisions, about 60,000 men. They would push west toward the big naval port of Portsmouth, Britain's premier naval base. A second landing would occur to the east along the coast near the towns of Rye, Bexhill, and Eastbourne. The first wave of two infantry divisions, with 250 tanks, would be followed by 2 armored divisions with hundreds more tanks. This assault would push north and east toward London. In the meantime, more troops, tanks, guns, and equipment would arrive at the bridgehead.

The divisions would fight their way inland, with some forces heading west toward Bristol and the Bristol Channel, while others struck toward Oxford and the Cotswolds. Other forces would envelop London, fight across the Medway River toward London. The end result: cut off London, cut the country in two, crush resistance, fight off counterattacks, and starve London into surrender without the need to fight for the metropolis, street by street.

The German armed forces began gathering invasion equipment from all over Europe: troop-carrying barges, tugboats for towing, special landing craft, plus new assault weapons. These included new underwater tanks and floating tanks that could be off-loaded in the water and make their way to the beaches right through the surf. They were waterproof at least long enough to reach land.

Huge railway guns in France began shelling Southern England in 1940 and did not stop for 4 years. It was hoped these big guns would protect the German landing craft from British warships.

British Reconnaissance planes recorded the buildup to invasion: 168 transport ships; 419 tugboats for towing; 1900 barges for ferrying troops and tanks; 1,600 motor launches; 1,800 planes, including bombers, fighters, and dive bombers. Hitler's directive was simple: eliminate the 'English Motherland' and stop it from waging war against Germany.

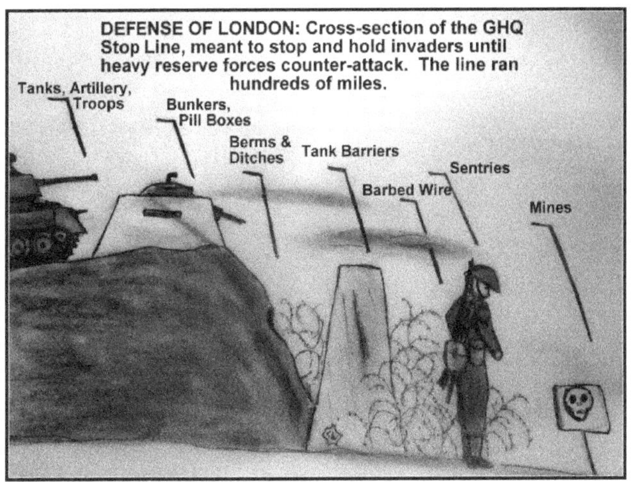

The SS and Security Service and Secret Police completed plans for the occupation of Britain. The headquarters of what would be a Police State would be in London. Dr. Franz Six would be in charge of the whole security apparatus including; special death squads; reprisals and hostage-taking for any resistance; the roundup of 'enemies' and those named in the Black Book; the 'final solution' for the Jews, and other harsh methods.

The Ministry of Information, located in the London skyscraper, Senate House, would be taken over. Many newspapers and magazines would be closed. The country would be stripped of valuables, industrial equipment, agricultural produce, and young men would be sent to Europe as forced labor. The country would be divided into six 'military-economic' districts, one of which would be London. In an attempt at irony, Hitler ordered that an overlord be appointed to rule Britain. His headquarters would be Blenheim Palace near Oxford, boyhood home of Churchill. Various names were put forward for the job, including Joachim Von Ribbentrop, German foreign minister and former ambassador to Britain. The planners even designated the luxury hotels and other buildings that would be confiscated to house the occupation government.

One of the main planners of the occupation was SS General Walter Schellenberg, aide to the deputy head of the SS, Reinhard Heydrich. It was Heydrich who ordered Schellenberg to prepare the lists of prominent Britons to be arrested. Later in the war, the British would enjoy sweet revenge. The Special Operations Executive, the British spy and sabotage agency, assisted the Czechs in assassinating Heydrich in Prague.

Schellenberg prepared a detailed analysis of British society, which he claimed was ruled by one-half of one percent of the population: graduates from the exclusive private schools, graduates of Oxford and Cambridge universities. At the end of the war, British troops captured Schellenberg and sent him for trial at Nuremburg. He spent five years in prison.

Hitler turned the first item on the invasion list over to his bombastic air force chief, Reichsmarschall Hermann Göring, a man of bravery, hubris and cruelty. The job: destroy the Royal Air Force and gain control of the skies. It would turn out to be a tall order. The Royal Air Force was short on fighter planes and pilots, but the ones it had were good. The country also had the capacity to build planes at a fast pace. Also, refugees from the conquered countries of Europe included a number of skilled pilots—Poles, Czechs, French, Belgian, and Dutch. They were eager to fight.

The German Air Force attacked the radar stations, air fields, command centers, and planes on the ground. Bombers struck airplane factories and engineering works. German submarines and lone-wolf battleships and cruisers hit shipping and blocked access to supplies and food sent by ship. The assault was intense. RAF fighters, the Spitfires and the Hurricanes, rose up to fight the bombers and their fighter escorts. Could they stop the onslaught from the air?

The first phase leading up to invasion had begun.

Britons Under the Nazis

In the meantime, the nation was getting a few hints about what would come with defeat and occupation. The Channel Islands—Jersey and Guernsey, located in the English Channel near France—were home to nearly 100,000 people, all subjects of the monarchy in London. It was decided not to defend the islands. Instead many people were evacuated, about 30,000. The Germans then arrived and occupied the islands without resistance.

At first, the occupation yoke was fairly light. The German commandant posted the rules:

- No resistance of any kind.
- 11 p.m. curfew.
- Confiscation of all weapons, guns, knives, and ammunition.
- No use of private cars.
- No boats to leave without permission.
- All prices frozen in place.
- No listening to radios except for German-controlled stations.
- Civil laws would continue, but military law would be the ultimate authority.

The Occupation Forces fortified the island as part of Hitler's Atlantic Wall. They built gun emplacements, concrete pillboxes and bunkers, and dug defensive tunnels into the cliffs. They brought in 16,000 forced laborers, including 1000 French Jews. The few Island Jews were persecuted and some sent to concentration camps.

At one point it was decided to confiscate all radios and censure or shut the newspapers. There was no outside news, although some secretly listened to the BBC. Some islanders resisted as best they could. Some islanders collaborated and fraternized with the enemy. Some engaged in sexual relations, which other islanders deeply resented.

The occupation was hard, but not as harsh as in many other places further east. Still, it was made clear that armed resistance would lead to deadly reprisals and collective punishment. Freedom left the islands.

Chapter 2
Total Mobilization

Churchill, his war cabinet, his generals, and admirals, were confronted with the greatest crisis in the nation's history, going back at least to William the Conqueror, the Spanish Armada, or Napoleon Bonaparte. Just across the channel was Hitler, his conquered lands, and his Italian ally, Mussolini. They could command 10 to 15 million soldiers and sailors, thousands of war planes; fleets of battleships, cruisers, and enough submarines to shut off all trade. They seemed to possess all the time, the money, and the power. They knew no restraints, and were willing to wage war in some sort of Darwinian frenzy—no mercy; the wasps attack the bees and destroy them down to the final buzz. The future belonged to the killers.

There was only one choice to be made in the face of total destruction or total surrender: Total mobilization; prepare for total war on all fronts and by all means. No one was exempt now, no one spared. The orders went out from London, from Downing Street and Whitehall: the nation mobilized to a degree perhaps not seen before. Every person in the country, men, women, and children would play a role. Few or no exemptions. Volunteer or be drafted into service. In the coming weeks and months, the nation was transformed:

- The Armed Services; Army, Navy, Air Force, and Royal Marines grew until they eventually numbered 5.5 million, including 445,000 women in the three women's branches, ATS, WAAF, and WRNS.
- A new defense force, the Home Guard, was formed for older men. It would grow quickly to 1.6 million members. It would fight house to house, street by street, if necessary. (Yes, women were enlisted.)

- Millions of men and women were enlisted into war work:
  Civil Defense, the fire and rescue brigades, air raid wardens, military auxiliaries for women, nursing corps, and war industries. Some two million worked in Air Raid Precaution, fire and rescue, police, and other services. Many were women.
- A new Women's Land Army marched out to increase food production.
- The London Metropolitan Police more than doubled, from 18,000 to 44,000, with reserves and auxiliaries.
- London was full of exiles and refugees. They formed their own fighting forces under an overall British command: the Poles, a corps of 40,000; Czechs, Dutch, and the Free French under Charles de Gaulle. From the Dominions, a Canadian infantry division arrived to be followed by others. Australians and New Zealanders rallied to the cause.
- New war agencies, such as the Special Operations Executive, enlisted women as special agents and even saboteurs.
- A critical role in the war effort fell to the Merchant Navy fleet, at the time the world's largest with 7,000 ships, and 190,000 sailors. They carried half the nation's food and all its oil. The need for manpower increased with losses, and 60,000 ex-seafarers were drafted into service. It was said the merchant seamen 'got no hero's salute, but they were on the front line'. They paid the price: 2400 ships sunk and 32,000 seamen killed.
- The Civil Service, numbering 664,000 members, ran dozens of alphabet agencies and worked as propagandists, clerks, food inspectors, and social workers. Their numbers were expected to grow as government took on more social welfare projects.

Almost all adults were subject to a draft, including women. In a report to Parliament, Ernest Bevin, Minister of Labor, said that women would have to take over much of the work formerly done by men, in fields and factories, shops and offices, as more men were called into the military. He added that nurseries, child care, and help for working mothers 'will become a state responsibility'.

In all 17 million people, a third of the nation, were in direct war work, in the military, the defense factories or fire protection and civil defense. Children were expected to do their part—go to school, or perhaps be evacuated from the cities. Several million were sent to the countryside or to villages. Even the elderly and the disabled were asked to play a role, however modest.

Regular civilian life seemed to cease. The government requisitioned trains, ports, private ships, luxury liners, hotels, golf courses, and even theaters. Hotels became hospitals and golf courses were made into airfields.

Gone were the posh lifestyles, the easy living, and the swanky surroundings of London life. Everything was more democratic now; the British class system began to break down. Restaurants became canteens, and everybody enjoyed a 'cuppa' tea. Movies were popular, and a staple became war films. The bands and orchestras played, but now it was for everyone. Exclusivity was out, at least for now.

The Dark Age

Anyone flying at night over London and Britain would have looked into vast darkness. Millions of buildings and houses were 'blacked-out' with special curtains drawn to let out no light that would guide and attract bombers. The blackouts would last for years, and much of Europe was blacked-out for that period. It was truly a dark age. Thousands of Air Raid Wardens enforced the blackouts. Most people were anxious to comply. There was a sense of social cohesion. It would not last when the crisis passed. Now it was, 'We're all in this together' and 'everyone needs to do their part.'

A famous poster urged: 'Keep Calm and Carry on.' Another poster called for:

'WOMEN OF BRITAIN,
COME INTO THE FACTORIES'

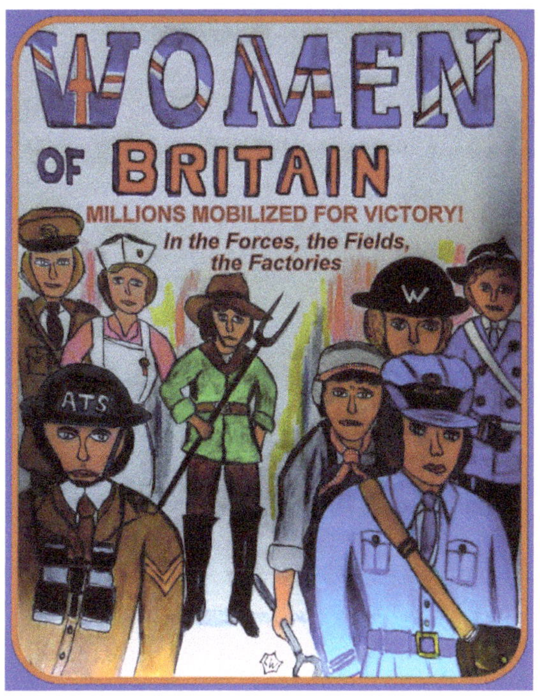

A top priority was to crank out as many fighter planes and bombers as possible. Churchill appointed Lord Beaverbrook, a Canadian-born press lord, to be minister of aircraft production. Plenty of women came into the factories to build the planes and the bombs they dropped.

Stop Line

Britain was fighting back. An air war raged over the country. This became known as *The Battle of Britain.* Day and night, squadrons of British fighters rose from their air fields to meet the waves of German bombers and fighter escorts. The Germans now were paying a price in lost planes and pilots. Could Britain hold on and hold out, and replace the planes and pilots it was losing?

The Germans had more planes, but the British developed an effective system of radar early warning, plane spotters, and control centers to track the incoming bombers. The fighters could then effectively intercept the enemy planes. It became an air war of attrition. Many days both sides lost scores of planes, hundreds in a week.

It was a grim time, and no one knew the outcome. Churchill, a Conservative, headed a coalition government of labor/socialists and other parties. Labor's Clement Atlee was the deputy prime minister. They all put aside partisan politics for now in the face of a threat to existence itself. Partisan infighting was a luxury of the good times. Peaceful times.

When he first came to power, Churchill gave a speech in Parliament that was broadcast to the nation. It was one of the most remarkable and chilling speeches a leader ever gave to his people. It would set the tone for the coming years. He told them they would have to sacrifice, fight, and even die for the country. In return, he could give them little or nothing.

"I have nothing to offer you but blood, toil, tears and sweat. We have before us an ordeal of the most grievous kind."

He went on to say that the goal was 'Victory. Without victory there is no survival.'

Some weeks later, the situation had deteriorated, and Churchill again spoke to the nation by way of Parliament. It has become one of the most famous speeches. This time, he raised the threat of invasion. He presented a plan—a grim plan—to fight off an invasion, with no certainty of success. He warned of the consequences of failure.

"Even though large tracts of Europe and many old and famous states have fallen under the grip of the Gestapo and all the odious apparatus of Nazi rule, we shall not flag or fail.

"We shall go on to the end. We shall fight in France. We shall fight on the seas and oceans. We shall fight with growing strength and growing confidence in the air, we shall defend our island whatever the cost may be. We shall fight on the beaches, we shall fight on the landing grounds, we shall fight in the fields and in the streets, we shall fight in the hills; we shall never surrender."

He added ominously that even if the nation, or a large part of it 'were subjugated and starving', the fight would continue in the Empire and the Dominions.

In an earlier speech, Churchill had said, *"We are told Herr Hitler has a plan for the invasion of this island. I would remind him what Napoleon's general told him at Boulogne: 'There are bitter weeds in England.'"*

The 'beaches' speech is often quoted. But what was the follow-up? What was done to implement the brave fighting words? The generals and admirals devised a plan to 'defend our island'. General Edmund Ironside was appointed overall commander of the home defense. In short order, he was replaced by General Alan Brooke, who was younger and deemed to be more familiar with the new style of warfare.

In broad terms, the plan against invasion entailed:

- Bomber attacks on the ports and staging areas in France, Belgium, and Holland to hinder the invasion buildup.
- On the beaches, all sorts of tank barriers, gun emplacements, pill boxes, mines, and barbed wire entanglements would slow or stop the invaders. Plans were laid to put pipes on the beaches and pump flaming liquids, oil and petroleum, in the path of the landing craft. The enemy would face a 'sea of flames'.

Poison Gas

General Brooke later revealed there was a plan to use airplanes to spray poison gas on the invading forces. This was an all-out war and survival was at stake. British forces stockpiled several kinds of poisonous gases, including mustard, phosgene, and chlorine.

- The Stop Lines. If the Germans established a beachhead, and started to fight their way inland, they would confront a series of 'stop lines'—heavily defended lines of guns, concrete bunkers, mine fields, tank barriers and traps, berms, booby traps, and pill boxes for cannons and machine guns.

The largest and most formidable of these was the GHQ Stop Line established in front of London. It ran for hundreds of miles across southern England and then swung northward.

The goal would be to slow down the invaders, who then would be hit by elite British forces held in reserve. This counterattack would be crucial.

Slowing the invasion would also give the Royal Navy time to send heavy warships, cruisers, destroyers, and subs into the invasion zone to block and destroy the ships and boats bringing supplies and re-enforcements. This was the biggest fear of the German planners. They could not match the Royal Navy's strength and firepower. The Home Fleet consisted of 80 ships, including 8 battleships. Much of the fleet was held in reserve some 600 miles north of London at Scapa Flow, a mooring off the coast of Scotland. Other ships were much closer, at Portsmouth and Plymouth.

Suicide Squads

British defenders devised all sorts of plans to slow and disrupt the invaders. They took down all street and road signs to add to the enemy's confusion.

They created hundreds of 'suicide squads',' small units attached to the Home Guard. The Special Operations Executive, the agency set up for 'irregular warfare' organized the teams. Each team would go underground, literally. They would hide out and emerge to fight the Germans from the rear. They were given ammunition and food to survive a few days or weeks at most. Members of the squads knew they would not survive. It was a suicide mission.

"We shall fight them in the fields and in the streets." That would be the job of the Home Guard, now 1.6 million strong. These older fighters, dubbed 'Dad's Army', played a secondary role patrolling and guarding roads, bridges, junctions, and looking for enemy spies and infiltrators. In an all-out invasion, they would be expected to 'guard the homes', fight the enemy, and resist at all cost.

They used 'improvised explosive devices' such as sticky bombs that could be slapped onto tanks and vehicles. Pipe bombs were buried or hidden, along with buried gasoline bombs. Bridges were rigged with explosives. Guardsmen learned how to make Molotov cocktails; the gasoline bombs made with bottles and rags.

British disinformation agents were busy. They circulated tales about new secret weapons that acted as giant flamethrowers. They put out a false story that the Germans had tried a trial landing on the coast and suffered disastrous casualties—a defeat that had been covered up, so it couldn't be denied.

The British military chiefs in London moved large defensive forces into Southern England, in a ring around London, and divided into five corps. Several dozen divisions and brigades of infantry, armor, and mobile forces provided a defense in depth. Some were grouped together as the GHQ reserves that would deliver a hammer-blow counterattack.

One key part of the defense were the Canadians, the 1st, 2nd, and 3rd Infantry Divisions, designated the First Canadian Army. They stood in Sussex in front of London to defend the 'mother country'. VII Corps, made up of British, Canadian and New Zealand troops, constituted a key part of the counter-attack force, and was anchored by the First Armored Division. The corps was commanded by a Canadian general. IV Corps, built around the 2nd Armored Division, was held back as a counter-attack force. Canadian forces arrived in 1939, fought in France, and would stay in Britain until 1944, after which they would participate in the liberation of Europe. Throughout these war years, some 330,000 Canadian personnel would pass through Britain. They would father 22,000 children.

Two Australian Army brigades served in the mobile reserve force guarding London. Australian fighter squadrons fought in air war; airmen and sailors served in the Royal Navy and RAF. Fully, 13,000 Aussie airmen served in the Fighter, Coastal, and Bomber Commands. More than 1,400 were shot down and captured.

New Zealand pilots flew with the RAF, and sailors served on navy ships. A New Zealander, Air Chief Marshal Sir Keith Park, commanded the air group protecting London. He was dubbed 'Defender of London' and a statue of him stands on Trafalgar Square. New Zealand prime minister, M. J. Savage, summed up the prevailing attitude as: "Where Britain stands, we stand."

Although it wasn't fully formed until later, the British Army's 56th (London) Infantry Division contained the London Irish Rifles, the 1st London Scottish Battalion, a battalion of the Scots Guards, and the Welsh Regiment. The division would later serve in Palestine, North Africa, Sicily, and Italy. Other Army units with London ties were the regiments of the County of London Yeomanry, which served in various armored divisions, including the 79th Armored Division.

One of the many Army units was the Artists' Rifles, made up of artists, writers, musicians, and actors. It had been formed 80 years before, and was now a part of the London Regiment. The Rifles served as a training regiment, but saw much action after the war in far-flung places.

To give better command and control, and foil enemy attempts to send fake orders, the British Army built its own radio station to broadcast orders and codes to troops and the Home Guard.

Bomber Command kept bombers at the ready to go into action when invasion came. The Home Fleet was ready to send ships into action or reposition them. If invasion was imminent, a prearranged coded signal would be sent out and all the defensive elements would go into action. Troops would move into position. The Home Guard would muster. The bombers would hit the invasion forces; the Navy ships would go into action.

Right in the invasion path west of London was Aldershot, the garrison town and headquarters of the British Army, home of the new paratrooper regiments, and training ground for the Free French Forces. Some 22,000 troops were stationed at Aldershot, many of them Canadians. Nearby was the Sandhurst Military College, Churchill's old war college, and the military aircraft research and development facilities at Farnborough where captured German planes were flown by the technocrats to test their capabilities.

The invaders would be striking at the heart of Britain's military establishment. Here 'home defense' would truly be personal.

Bunker

Because of the obvious aerial threat, the government and military leadership moved underground, into the heavily fortified underground Cabinet War Rooms located in the heart of Whitehall, the government district.

The bunker, located under the New Public Offices, a massive office building now housing the Treasury, was close to the Prime Minister's residence in Downing Street and the Houses of Parliament. The offices were capped with five feet of concrete. Even so the location was kept secret. The Germans possessed some massive bunker-busting bombs, 5,000 pound super bombs.

The War Rooms contained space for the prime minister, his deputies, the war cabinet, military chiefs, a map room, switchboard and communication center, and basic living quarters, dormitories, sleeping quarters as well as a bedroom and office for the prime minister. There were also facilities for live radio broadcasts, and a special room that held a private phone line linking Churchill with American President Franklin Roosevelt. The War Rooms operated 24 hours a day for 6 years.

It could house a staff of 528. Churchill spent much of the war in the bunker. The war cabinet met 115 times.

There were backup bunkers, including a top secret new underground facility, code-named Paddock, beneath the Post Office Research Station in North West London. It held 40 rooms. It was seldom used.

The most formidable facility was right in the heart of the Whitehall government district. The Admiralty Citadel was part bunker, part fortress, and could have served as a last-ditch redoubt in an invasion. It was capped by 20 feet of concrete. It is still there today by Horse Guards Parade, a grim monument to total war.

Security for Churchill and his top deputies was a major concern. He had access to three country getaway mansions. Chequers, the estate 41 miles north of Central London, was given as a gift to the nation as a retreat for the prime minister. The security people balked at its use. Its entrance and roadway were easily seen from the air. Churchill's own country house, Chartwell in Kent, was in easy range of German planes. It sat on high ground nearly 700 feet above sea level. Its large grounds, 19 bedrooms and dressing rooms, and heated swimming pool went unused.

Churchill did use the more secure Ditchley House in Oxfordshire, which was loaned to him by an Anglo-American, Ronald Tree, who also was in Parliament. This house was hidden away by trees.

Late in 1942, the road approach to Chequers was camouflaged and Churchill returned there.

Invading Ireland

British war planners had to look west toward that Emerald Isle across the Irish Sea.

The Republic of Ireland declared itself neutral in the war. The reality was somewhat more complicated. Ireland had gained independence from London a couple of decades before. Irish Prime Minister Eamon de Valera and many Irish leaders had fought against British rule. Those same leaders watched as Hitler rolled over small countries, occupied them and used them to launch attacks against neighbors. Suddenly Irish independence seemed fragile.

For the British, the reality went beyond German invasion of Britain. What if Hitler invaded and seized Ireland and outflanked Britain, caught it in a vise from East and West? The British drew up plans for the invasion of Ireland. In two of the three contingencies, the Irish government offered cooperation.

- The Doomsday Scenario: Britain is invaded and conquered. British forces retreat to Ireland and continue to fight. The Irish agree to coordinate with the British and offer base locations. This willingness to drop neutrality stemmed from the realization that if Britain was conquered, Ireland would lose its independence as surely as did Holland, Belgium, Norway, and Denmark.
- As the blockade grows more intense and desperation sets in, the British determine they must use southern Irish ports, Cork and Cobh. They seize the ports by force, if the Irish government resists.
- The Germans invade Ireland. This triggers a British invasion of Ireland to block the Germans. That invasion would come from Northern Ireland, British territory bordering the Republic.

The British and Irish coordinate plans to fight the German invasion. The 'neutrality' stance is preserved by stipulating the British will only intervene when 'invited in' by the Irish prime minister.

The plan is elaborate and code-named *Plan W*. British Intelligence estimates a German invasion by sea and air would involve 100,000 top-line troops, including paratroopers.

They would likely attack around port cities in the south and west. They would be met by Irish troops, and the small Irish navy and air force. The British would invade from the north with heavy army divisions, squadrons of the Royal Air Force, warships, and a supply system involving trains from the Belfast area moving troops and supplies into the Irish Republic. A steady stream of ships from Scottish and English ports would constantly resupply the forces as they battle the German invaders.

Even with the cooperation of Dublin, it was feared the Irish patriots would resist invading British even if it was to fight the Germans. British forces would be careful with the use of symbols, flags, and signs that suggested any return to British rule.

The Germans looked at an Irish invasion but never followed through. During the war, the Irish quietly cooperated with the British in a number of ways, by providing weather information, shipping food, repairing ships, arresting spies, and allowing British military access to remote regions of Ireland.

The Irish government looked the other way as more than 50,000 Irish citizens joined the British military, and thousands more traveled to England to work in the war effort. In a bit of irony, more Irish Republic citizens fought in the British forces than did those from Northern Ireland, which did not have a draft.

A little less than 40,000 Northern Irish served in the forces, although Northern Ireland built warships and planes and provided foodstuffs, port facilities, and was a major staging ground for American troops. A draft was ruled out for fear of antagonizing the often anti-British Catholic minority.

Some 36,000 sailors of the Royal Navy, the Canadian Navy and the U.S. Navy were stationed at Londonderry, Northern Ireland during the Battle of the Atlantic.

The German embassy in Dublin stayed open throughout the war. The ambassador, Eduard Hempel, sent thousands of messages and reports to Berlin, but the embassy was not a center of espionage, as the British feared. A report to Parliament at the end of the war pointed out that there were only nine staffers in the embassy, the majority of them clerks.

De Valera stirred great controversy when late in the war in Europe he paid a visit to the embassy to offer condolences after Hitler died of suicide in his Berlin bunker.

Ireland was not considered to be one of the victorious Allies.

The Black Move

Whatever happened to Ireland hardly mattered if Britain itself was lost. If the invaders were winning and about to capture London, occupy it or destroy it, government plans called for the so-called Black Move. The government would abandon the city and relocate to pre-planned locales around the country. Parliament would relocate to Stratford-upon-Avon, Shakespeare's town. The prime minister would go to Spetchley Park, a 4,500 acre estate near the city of Worcester, more than a

100 miles northwest of London. Some 16,000 state workers and the war cabinet would move to nearby Hindlip Hall, a large estate. The Royal Family, including princesses Elizabeth and Margaret, would go to Madresfield Court, a stately home at Malvern in the Worcestershire Hills.

Some private businesses moved out of London on their own. The London, Midland and Scottish Railway, with 270,000 employees, moved its headquarters and 3,000 staff to Hertfordshire in just 3 days. National art treasures and gold reserves needed to be removed to safer places; the gold, 65 million ounces, was moved to Canada.

Government functions were already being dispersed to coastal towns and spa towns with big hotels. Some 23,000 civil servants were sent out of London. The BBC and the Post Office moved some functions to other cities.

The treasures of the vast British Museum, which also included millions of books, stamp collections, and priceless objects spanning the history of mankind, were dispersed to an unused tube station, basements, and locations in Wales.

Among the treasures moved out: the Elgin marbles from the Greek Parthenon; the Rosetta Stone, the Magna Carta, the Gutenberg Bibles, and the Lindesfarne Illuminated Gospels. The move saved a lot of the artifacts. The museum was bombed. The grand Duveen Gallery, which housed the Elgin marbles was wrecked. The Victoria and Albert Museum, with its 125 galleries, moved its treasures underground, to a rock quarry in Wiltshire and to an estate in the west of England. The museum was turned into classrooms and a canteen for the Royal Air Force.

The National Gallery of Art considered sending its hundreds of paintings to Canada. Prime Minister Churchill ordered that no paintings should leave the country. Instead they were sent to colleges and a castle in Wales. Many were sent to an underground rock quarry at Manod in the Welsh mountains where they were held at a constant temperature, a move that turned out to be beneficial in preserving the paintings. The empty National Gallery mounted music recitals and small art exhibits despite the bombing. Pianist Myra Hess organized more than 1,700 music events, including 150 where she played.

The Tate Gallery of British Art, home to the works of Turner, Constable, Whistler and the 19th Century Pre-Raphaelite painters, was emptied out, with paintings stored underground. One painting, too large to move, was protected by a special brick wall. The gallery was badly damaged in the bombing.

Gas Attack

Before war broke out, government officials studied the likely effect on London and other cities hit by modern warfare and aerial bombing. The predictions were grim. Casualties could be in the millions, estimates said.

Poison gas had been used in World War I. There was no reason not to assume its use again. Government officials ordered the production of 50 million gas masks, including special gas hoods for infants. The Ministry of Health drew up plans to evacuate millions from the cities. Many children were evacuated.

Churchill, the Terrorist?

The German air assault continued. Again, the targets were military and industrial. There was no concerted effort to bomb civilians. There were incidents when civilians were hit.

Then an event occurred that would change the whole course of the war, and the course of history. Churchill, incensed by the ceaseless air attacks on the homeland, demanded that the RAF Bomber Command hit Germany.

On August 25, 1940, a wave of 95 British planes took off for the first night bombing raid on Berlin, a sprawling target and home to 4.5 million people. Just 81 planes got through to the targets, Templehof Airport, and the industrial complex of Siemenstadt. The attack was not effective and did little damage. Some civilians were killed.

The psychological impact was immense. Germans had attacked dozens of foreign cities. Now its capital was under fire. The leader, *Der Fuhrer*, was not perfect, and not able to protect the capital city.

Hitler was furious. He spoke to the faithful at the Berlin Sportpalast. He accused Churchill of being ‘a terrorist’. He warned that his bombers would ‘erase London’. He said bombs dropped on Germany would be paid back one hundredfold.

His next order changed the war and probably changed history. He ordered that the Luftwaffe turn its bombers toward London and other cities. London would be the main target, and now civilians would be hit.

Up to this point, the air assault aimed to knock out the RAF, its bases, radars, aircraft factories, and other strategic targets. Air Force chief Göring said the new bombing strategy is to 'drive eight million Londoners insane'.

On September 7, 1000 German planes, bombers, and fighters attacked London's East End, with bombers returning day and night. It was called *Operation Loge*, after the Nordic god of fire.

A London Fire Brigade official looked out at the docks that fed, fueled and financed London's millions. A wall of flames spread across three miles. He called for 500 fire trucks. Another official, skeptical of the order, rushed to look. He called for a 1000 fire trucks.

Now began the London Blitz, which did not spare other British cities. For the next nine months, the bombing raids would go on day and night. There would be 267 days of attacks. London was hit for 57 nights in a row.

In London, a million homes would be damaged or destroyed, and 20,000 people killed. Thousands more were hurt.

These were 'terror-angriffs'—terror attacks. They were made without regard for the civilian population. In fact, the attacks from the air would continue for 5 years until 1945. Still to come would be a rain of thousands of rockets and missiles.

Is London Burning?

On the night of December 29, London was hit with what became known as the 'Second Great London Fire'. The Luftwaffe dropped 24,000 bombs and 100,000 fire-starting incendiaries. Some 1,500 fires raged, many of them out of control. Nineteen churches were destroyed. The Fire Brigade lost 14 men, and 250 were injured.

Churchill ordered that St. Paul's Cathedral, in the center of the bombing, be saved at all cost. Some 200 special 'fire watchers' were on duty to douse any fires started at the Christopher Wren masterpiece.

That night produced one of the great photographs of the war. As the fires raged in the night, press photographer Herbert

Mason stepped onto the roof of a building. There amid the smoke and flame of Dante's Inferno stood the mighty dome of St. Paul's, noble and seemingly untouched by the onslaught.

He took the picture that would come to represent London in the Blitz, a city grand, aloof, and unbeatable.

Another iconic photo, taken by a London fireman, during an earlier raid, showed the whole façade—several floors of the building at 23 Queen Victoria Street crashing to the ground.

This was the international headquarters of the Salvation Army, the worldwide charity and church founded in East London in 1865.

The Luftwaffe had some monster bombs in the arsenal: 4,000-pound 'max' bombs; and the hellish 5,500-pound Satan bomb. These bombs could take down buildings and city blocks.

The incendiary bombs set fires that could build into firestorms. The incendiaries burned at 5,000 °F. The most common bomb was the SC-50, a 50-pound bomb carrying TNT. It blasted buildings and hurled shrapnel with metal shards traveling at 7,000 miles per hour. A Heinkel bomber carried 40 of these.

Bigger bombs were the killer, SC-500 and SC-1,000.

In addition to explosions, fires, collapse, and shrapnel was the so-called 'blast lung'. Bomb blasts and shock waves could suck the air out of a person's lungs, destroying the organ, and causing suffocation. They died with no obvious wounds.

The Fire Brigades and auxiliary firefighters faced new dilemmas from mass bombing of houses, warehouses, factories, gas tanks, and rail cars. On the same night they might have to fight chemical fires, rubber tire fires, conflagrations of munitions, petroleum, and even rum, alcohol or warehouses full of food. In one case a warehouse filled with black pepper burned, with stinging results.

London resisted and fought back. Londoners headed for bomb shelters and the safety of the subway tunnels when the sirens sounded the warning. Air raid wardens enforced a blackout, no lights showing, to make it hard for the bombers to locate targets.

To make it even harder, the defenders built fake cities in fields, with lights, sparking streetcars, and fires that looked like these were targets.

German bombers navigated with radio beams. The British broadcast competing beams to throw off the planes. This became known as 'the battle of the beams'.

German bombers navigated with radio beams. The British broadcast competing beams to throw off the planes. This became known as 'the battle of the beams'.

Anti-aircraft guns and searchlights tracked the planes. Many of these guns and lights were operated by women. These defenses forced the planes to fly higher and hurt their accuracy. In many cases gunners were ordered to fill the sky with firing just to show the public the city was fighting back.

Barrage balloons, tethered to the ground with cables, also forced the planes to stay higher. They could not risk flying low and clipping the balloons or cables. The beleaguered city carried on. Thousands of children were sent out into the villages and countryside for safety. London was full of soldiers, sailors, police and firemen, fire and rescue workers, and civil servants. Every other person seemed to be in uniform.

Women worked as firefighters, fire watchers, and formed Supplementary Fire Parties. Each party carried hand pumps and sand buckets and guarded groups of 30 houses.

Other men and women served on the rescue squads. One woman reported that when she arrived at her first bombed house, she confronted a baby blown to pieces in the street. She kept calm and covered it with a bed sheet.

Another woman, who admitted she was horrified by the sight of a dead animal, now drove an ambulance. She arrived at scenes of death and carnage and found she could handle the trauma. Women ran many of the services provided by the large charitable organizations, the YMCA, the Salvation Army, and the Red Cross. They provided bombed-out Londoners with food, clothing, and emergency shelter. One rescue worker remembers seeing an old woman, sitting in the ruins of her house, weeping uncontrollably. The old woman, still crying, wandered away into the ruined neighborhood. What would become of her, she wondered?

For most Londoners, life was a mixture of fear, excitement, boredom, tedium, and long working hours, with not enough sleep or palatable food. For thousands of civil defense workers, death and injury were a real possibility.

All fire, rescue, police, air raid wardens and ambulance workers wore steel helmets marked with their jobs: R for Rescue, W for Warden. There were 42 different civil defense jobs with helmet markings; they were needed. London was rich in targets. At the London Royal Arsenal, 32,500 workers made and filled bombs, and fashioned fuses. The arsenal was hit 25 times, either by bombs or missiles. Some 800 workers were killed or wounded. Much of the work was dispersed to other arsenals, but despite the danger 18,000 workers stayed on.

The Royals Naval College at Greenwich, which was bombed several times, still managed to train 35,000 Naval officers, men and women, during the war.

Malice Toward the Palace

The great state institutions, symbols of power and authority were hit, and then hit again: the Buckingham Palace and the Palace of Westminster, home to the House of Commons and House of Lords. Kensington Palace was hit by incendiaries and partially burned. Buckingham Palace was hit seven times, and one raid destroyed the Royal Chapel. These scenes were shown in movie theaters to indicate the King and Queen were suffering with the commoners.

The Royal Family would suffer even more, with a great personal loss. The King's younger brother, Prince George, Duke of Kent, known as the 'gallant and handsome prince', and a RAF pilot and air commodore on active service, was killed in a military plane crash in Scotland while flying to Iceland on a 'special mission'. He had become a father just seven weeks before the crash. He was buried with honors at Windsor Castle, with a dozen exiled kings, queens, crown princes, and other royalty in attendance.

Westminster Palace—the Parliament—was bombed 14 times. The Big Ben clock tower was hit but kept on ticking. The equestrian statue of King Richard the Lionheart was damaged and his sword bent. This prompted the saying, 'bent but not broken'.

Then on the night of May 10, 1941, true disaster struck. A heavy bomb crashed through the roof of the House of Commons. The explosion and flames threatened to destroy the venerable legislative body. Then the flames burst into an even more historic space, the 1000-year-old Westminster Hall, one of Europe's most famous structures, with its oak hammer-beam ceiling. The Hall was the place of notorious trials of St. Thomas More and Guy Fawkes; site of royal ceremonies and state funerals.

Walter Elliot, an army colonel, former cabinet member and member of the House of Commons rushed to the building. After consulting with the Fire Brigade, he was told both the Commons and the Hall could not be saved. He ordered them to save Westminster Hall, which they did. The House of Commons could not be saved.

The prime minister's house, 10 Downing Street, was hit or damaged a number of times. The rambling house, which was the official residence, offices, and meeting place of the cabinet, was in the center of the government district, surrounded by massive office blocks housing the war office, Home Office, and cabinet departments. The entrance area of No. 10 was barricaded, sand-bagged, and guarded by police, Royal Marines, and the Home Guard.

On October 14, 1940, Churchill and his wife were dining in the Garden Rooms at No. 10. Suddenly, the area was shaken by a series of explosions. One blast killed three members of the Home Guard.

'On a providential impulse, I ordered the kitchen evacuated,' he wrote later.

A massive explosion destroyed the kitchen and damaged other areas of the house. A special bunker was then built at the house. The house was protected by steel plates, but these could not withstand a direct hit. A far more secure bunker, the Cabinet War Rooms, was close by. At one point, King George VI, who was visiting at No. 10, had to be taken into the bunker for safety.

Churchill usually stayed in one of the bunkers at night. Sometimes at night, he would go to the roof of the New Public Offices building and watch the air raids.

He worked at 10 Downing Street in the day, and made a point of being photographed entering and leaving the residence. He flashed the 'V for Victory' sign. He wanted to be seen unafraid and not hunkered down in the bowels of the city.

Even in this 'darkest hour', there were talks and debates in Parliament about 'war aims' and what would happen when the war ended.

Sir Charles Mander, in a triumph of optimism over reality, speculated about a day when 'British and Allied troops will be on the streets of German cities so there will be no doubt they were defeated.'

Contrary to Reichsmarschall Göring's prediction, Londoners did not go crazy. The bombing did not destroy morale or willingness to fight. A couple of national organizations monitored public opinion. Mass Observation used hundreds of 'observers' who watched and listened and kept notes on how people acted and what they said. These were compiled into reports. MO did not find mass hysteria or mass depression. Most people soldiered on. Some were more worried about their pets than themselves. They had good reason to be.

Pet Armageddon

Pets suffered terribly in the bombing. Suddenly, the pets were liabilities. The government put out the word pets would not be allowed in shelters. Some 50 million gas masks were produced for people, none for animals. Who would take care of the pets in the chaos and homelessness? Who would feed the pets when there's rationing and food shortages? Authorities claimed dogs ate millions of pounds of meat a year, and cats consumed fish and 40 million gallons of milk.

Many pet owners panicked. A great wave of pet euthanasia swept across the city and the land. It was a mass culling. Many owners thought they were being humane. Others let pets loose in the streets, particularly cats.

The London Zoo in Regents Park, fearful the bombing would let loose dangerous animals, had some carnivores, deadly reptiles, and certain spiders euthanized. Others were saved, including a komodo dragon and Chinese alligators. Pythons were fitted with their own protective boxes. Some animals were moved to a countryside zoo. Camels and llamas were put to work as pack animals. Food was in short supply. Fish disappeared, and the pelicans had to be persuaded to eat meat coated with fish liver oil.

The zoo was bombed. A zebra ran loose in Camden Town. The Camel House was hit but the camels remained calm and unfazed. The zoo remained open. People 'adopted' animals to help with the feeding. Wounded soldiers got in free. The first woman zoo keeper went to work. Churchill and his wife Clementine visited the zoo in the war years. A photograph shows them holding a lion cub.

A Piggery in the Park

Hyde Park, the city's largest green space and the 'lungs of London', became a large potato patch, and site for anti-aircraft guns and searchlights. Sheep grazed. The police set up a 'piggery' and raised pigs. Authorities dug bomb shelters—some 66 bombs fell on the park.

London Underground

As the bombs fell, London went underground. Government policy ruled out the use of the subway, the Underground, for bomb shelters. The people themselves changed that. They began to show up at the stations with food and bedding. Police and officials stood aside. Discarded, too, was the fear of creating a 'bunker mentality' that would make people afraid to come out of the shelters.

The government began to outfit stations and tunnels with bunk beds, chemical toilets, food canteens, and wardens to keep order. In short order there were 177,000 people sleeping in the Underground nightly. With the trains shut down, they even slept next to the normally electrified third rails.

It was obvious everyone could not shelter in the subways. The government built 8 huge shelters beneath the subway lines, shelters that could hold up to 8,000 people each. Public buildings with basements and cellars were designated public shelters. For instance, some 2,000 people sheltered nightly in the hulking Methodist Central Hall near Westminster Abbey.

The larger solution came in the form of home shelters. The most used were the Anderson Shelters, named after the government official who first suggested them. These could be set up at home, typically in the garden or yard. These were made of sheets of corrugated stainless steel that formed walls and a roof, placed four feet in the ground and covered with a foot and a half of earth. They could sleep as many as six people. Many Anderson shelters were provided free, and some 3.6 million were deployed.

Local governments promoted their use by saying: "The Council appeals to you to make a serious endeavor to erect your own shelter." They became a source of humor. *A Punch* cartoon showed a boy dancing on top of a shelter. His mother warns, 'Don't dance about on it, Winnie, you might fall through.' Another cartoon showed a family growing watermelons on top of their shelter.

Another home shelter, the Morrison shelter, named after Herbert Morrison, the Home Secretary, was small and meant to be used inside the house. This was basically a steel box that could be assembled at home from a kit. A heavy steel roof, with steel posts and wire mesh sides, was really just a super-strong table. People sheltered beneath the steel top. Some 600,000 of these were deployed.

None of the home shelters could survive a direct hit. They could protect from shock waves and debris from a near hit. A check of 136 bombed houses with Morrison shelters showed that 85% of the people survived.

Even the deep shelters could not guarantee safety. In 1940, a bomb hit the street above Bank Underground Station in the Financial District. The street fell into the station, killing 56 people.

Also in 1940 a 3,000-pound semi-armor piercing bomb hit the street above Balham Station in Wandsworth, London. The explosion and roof collapse killed 66 people and injured 70.

No place was perfectly safe. Selfridges Department Store on Oxford Street, the city's second largest department store, had a series of deep basements and sub-basements. The deepest was 200 feet below the street. In 1942, the U.S. Army moved a communications center into the deep basement that provided a secure telex link with the Pentagon and the White House, and also facilitated conversations between President Roosevelt and Churchill. Some 50 Signal Corps personnel operated the center. The department store had been bombed several times, with considerable damage. Then in 1944, a V-2 Rocket slammed into the area above the deep shelter. This killed 8 American servicemen and wounded 32.

The worst incident happened in 1943. The RAF had hit Berlin with a major bombing run, and London was bracing for a retaliatory raid. When air raid sirens sounded, 1,500 people rushed to Bethnal Green Tube Station in East London. At the same time explosions were heard, which came from an experimental British rocket system. Whether panic set in or someone fell at the bottom of the stairs has never been determined. People at the bottom were trampled, with 173 deaths, including 62 children. News of the disaster was delayed 36 hours, and the exact details were kept secret for morale purposes.

The Communist Party, which was growing in numbers, was critical of the government's shelter policies, and linked them to indifference to the working class and its safety. The party newspaper, *The Daily Worker*, was accused of undermining the war effort.

A Touch of Class

Britain's class system didn't fade away in the face of deadly warfare, or the democracy of the shelters. The great luxury hotels of Mayfair, Knightsbridge, Piccadilly, and the Strand remained places of privilege and relative comfort.

The plush *Dorchester* Hotel, Park Lane, Mayfair was preferred by those of the ruling class seeking a classier bomb shelter. The hotel was built with re-enforced concrete with a huge basement. It was billed as bombproof. The famous and the well-connected felt comfortable here. Lord Halifax, when he was foreign secretary, kept eight rooms and the chapel. General Dwight D. Eisenhower, the American supreme commander, kept a suite here. Air Chief Marshal Portal of the RAF stayed here, as did several cabinet members.

The *Savoy* in the Strand, a hotel organized by Cesar Ritz and Chef Auguste Escoffier back in 1889, claimed its air raid shelter was the 'smartest in London'. The Americans loved the hotel, and Churchill brought his cabinet here regularly for lunch. The hotel did suffer from the bombing, the rationing, the shortage of staff, and the limits put on prices. Still, it kept up an appearance of luxury.

The *Hotel Claridge's*, haunt of kings, queens, and prime ministers, housed the exiled Yugoslavians, including King Peter II.

The *Hotel Ritz* on Piccadilly remained open even though it was damaged nine times by bombing. The Albanian royal family, headed by King Zog I, took over an entire floor. The royal jewels were put in the Bank of England. Many famous people favored the Ritz, which was famous for its elaborate afternoon teas. The basement bar was a safe hideaway for London's gay and lesbian community.

The grand but discreet *Connaught Hotel* in Mayfair was the wartime home of General de Gaulle, leader of the Free French and future French president. The hotel had been called the Coburg after the German royal house of Saxe-Coburg. In World War I it was changed to Connaught after the Duke of Connaught, son of Queen Victoria, when a German name no longer seemed appropriate. The British royal family also changed its name, from the German Saxe-Coburg to Windsor, after the town and its royal castle.

The Grosvenor House Hotel in Mayfair was protected by 10,000 sand bags and miles of blackout material to cover windows. The Great Room, which could hold 2,000 people, was used as an officers' club, and later as a mess hall for American officers.

Out of Joint

The grand restaurants had a harder time. *Simpson's-in-the-Strand*, the quintessential British restaurant with its joints of beef and mutton on trolleys waiting to be carved represented what humorist P. G. Wodehouse called 'the god of fatted plenty'. Rationing changed all that. The fine cuts of beef disappeared. The restaurant did get in some venison and smoked herring, but the government put on price ceilings in restaurants. Meals could not cost more than 5 shillings, about $16 in current money. No gourmet dining on that.

Rules in Covent Garden, another bastion of British cookery, with thick meats, old cheeses on the board, and claret and cigars, was hurt badly by rationing and price controls. It stayed open—two hours a day, from 1 to 3 p.m. It did get around the rationing by serving game, rabbits, grouse and pheasants which were not covered by the rules.

Restaurants did try to stay open despite the drawbacks and dangers. That included some gems, such as *Criterion* where the fictional Sherlock Holmes and Dr. Watson met for the first time; and the elegant *Café Royal*. *Quaglino's* in St. James's, famous for its supper club orchestra and entertainment, remained a place to see and be seen. *Restaurant Maxim*, another supper club, remained popular. *Veeraswamy* on Regent Street had the distinction of being the first restaurant serving dishes from India. There would be many more.

Then there were the pubs with their pub grub. The famous *Ye Olde Cheshire Cheese* on Fleet Street, which had hosted Charles Dickens, Arthur Conan Doyle, and legions of ink-stained journalists, was spared bomb damage. Perhaps it was protected by the sign, which stated, 'Rebuilt in 1667, the year of the Great London Fire.'

More in line with ordinary folks were the *Lyons' Corner House Cafes*, a popular chain of rambling restaurants on multiple floors. They served breakfast, light lunches, afternoon teas, dinners, and provided live entertainment, gifts, candies, sweets, and flowers. Some stayed open 24 hours a day. Lyons' was famous for its waitresses, women in white caps and aprons who were called Nippies. They became a kind of local institution. They were a comforting sight along with the comfort food. It was claimed that hundreds of Nippies married customers each year.

The great trans-Atlantic Cunard luxury liners, *Queen Mary* and *Queen Elizabeth,* were pressed into service as troop transports. In 1942, *Queen Mary* sailed from New York to Britain with 16,000 American troops, the most people ever to sail on a ship.

The damage and deaths from bombings, though considerable, were not as great as had been predicted in pre-war planning, which had foreseen the possibility of casualties in the millions. The tube system saved lives. One tunnel contained an entire airplane factory stretching for two miles. A small railway track was used to service the factory line.

People lived and died in the shelters. Some were born there. American television celebrity Jerry Springer was born in 1944 in High Gate Underground Station. His mother had taken shelter there from German rocket attacks. Springer's parents were Jewish refugees from Germany. They would later move to the United States.

The Good Life Ends

There was great deprivation. Private consumption plummeted. No cars, no tires, no luxuries. Many people were 'bombed out' of their homes. Everything was rationed, especially food. People were issued ration books that determined how much they could obtain.

There was a certain democracy of deprivation. J. B. Priestley, the writer and playwright, gave a regular talk on radio after the evening national news. The talks gained an audience of millions. Priestly saw a new kind of war and a new kind of soldier. This was a 'people's war, a citizen's war'.

"We are being bombed and burned into democracy," he said. "We're not really civilians any longer but a mixed bag of soldiers—milkmen and postmen soldiers, housewife and mother soldiers." He added, "We are being banged in the middle of the world stage."

Life went on for those on or off the stage. For John, a nine-year-old boy in the West London suburbs, not even war could dim the wonder and newness of youth. He saw the bombing, the Blitz, the searchlights scanning the sky, the rush of people to shelters, the marching troops, the daily grind for his family and friends faced with fear, broken by moments of elation.

He remembered. As an adult, John—John Boorman—would turn all this into a movie, *Hope and Glory*, which would gain several Academy Award nominations.

The movie pictured what he saw:

- Troops chasing down a runaway barrage balloon bouncing off the rooftops.
- A German pilot, his plane shot down, parachutes into a garden, sits down, smokes a cigarette as residents gather around him with non-threatening curiosity, and waits for the police to arrive.
- Children play, fight, and romance in the bombed-out houses. They make the best of the bad hand dealt to them.

A Sinking Feeling

Britain had to import half its meat, 70% of cheese and sugar, and 80% of fresh fruit.

German U-boats and surface ships began to sink British supply ships by the hundreds. The carnage would continue until the convoy system of many ships moving together and guarded by warships curtailed the losses. Some food shipments did get through, from the U.S. and Canada. Bombing of rail lines, train yards, ports, and warehouses further restricted supplies.

Gasoline for private use disappeared. Lemons and bananas could not be found. Food rationing was controlled by the Ministry of Food.

Each week a citizen could obtain a maximum of:

- Bacon or ham: 8 oz.
- Cheese: 8 oz.
- Sugar: 16 oz.
- Butter: 8 oz.
- Loose tea: 4 oz.
- Eggs: 1 egg.
- Preserves 1 lb./ month

A communal restaurant offered simple meals, and limited choices, but low prices. Here's an example:

Scotch broth.
Fried cod and chips.
Grilled sausage and mash.
Steak pie and two veg.
Roast lamb.
Macaroni and cheese.
Boiled potato greens
Rhubarb tart and custard.
Rice pudding.
Blancmange with jelly

Britain was forced to fight a war on a diet of vegetables, grains, potatoes, and coarse bread. Research that was kept secret indicated people would survive without imports, but with a dull, morale-shattering diet that produced prodigious amounts of gas—flatulence. A fart diet. Many people grew their own food on home plots, in gardens, and allotments. Some kept game birds.

The Women's Land Army opened up new land for food production. The Ministry of Food tried to make meals more palatable with new and novel ways to use potatoes, vegetables, and grains. Most recipes were met with less than enthusiasm.

Among the most famous—or infamous—concoctions was the 'national loaf', which replaced popular white bread with a loaf of coarse wholemeal brown bread. Another affront to gastronomy was the 'Woolton Pie', named after Frederick Marquis, Earl of Woolton, the Minister of Food. It was a mélange of carrots, potatoes, turnips, and oatmeal baked in a pastry or potato crust and served with brown gravy.

One member of Parliament proposed the government develop and distribute a special biscuit with ten vitamins plus iron, calcium and other minerals. The spokesman for the Ministry of Food said that while there didn't seem to be a need, the agency would 'take it under advisement'.

The government promoted a 'milk scheme' of subsidized milk for infants, young children, and mothers that reached 3.5 million people. School meals were expanded.

Food consumption was a touchy subject. Robert Boothby, parliamentary secretary for the Ministry of Food, refused to tell Parliament specific consumption figures. He said the numbers 'ought to be kept secret in time of war.' Why tell the Germans the effects of the blockade?

Restaurant meals were restricted and prices controlled. This was a social-leveling strategy to keep the rich from dining well while others consumed coarse bread and rationed butter, and 'Woolton Pie'.

Many communities opened so-called 'British Restaurants' where anyone could dine for a low price. Food became an obsession, and food fairness an obsession within the obsession. The city of Birmingham complained about a shortage of beer.

"How can we expect working men to do the necessary work of war without their beer?" asked one official. "Beer is nourishment for working people."

Others promoted the sale of soft drinks on the theory that soft beverages would stave off overindulgence in hard liquor and alcohol in general.

There was a candy crisis as sugar became scarce. "In Newcastle," said one lawmaker, "children are wandering around with pennies in their hand, unable to buy sweets of any description."

The presence of fresh oranges in London's Covent Garden made news. They had come in from South Africa.

One official complained that there was a shortage of meat and cheese in Glasgow. Another complained of a shortage of eggs in a northeastern town. The spokesman for the Ministry of Food was not encouraging: "There is a general shortage of eggs throughout the country."

People were discouraged from throwing rice at weddings. Why waste food on a ceremony?

The rationing controversy included horses. One woman Parliamentarian wanted to know why race horses were allotted 15 pounds of corn a day when working people were forced to kill their chickens because they could not feed them. The answer: Horse racing stock is a national asset and contributor to trade and exports.

Rations for horses were set according to their size and the type of work they did. These were heavy work horses, town horses, pack horses, riding horses, ponies, military horses. The rations in cereal grains ranged from 9 to 15 pounds a day per horse.

Plow the Hills

Every effort was made to boost food production, including some that generated plenty of controversy. The Minister of Agriculture was given new powers to open new land for food, including golf courses, sports fields, and parks.

Far more controversial were the War Agriculture Committees set up around the country. They had the power to evaluate farmers and kick them off their land until after the war was over unless they showed they used best practices and produced adequate crops. It was life or death for the nation, so the argument went, and the experts decided who stayed on the land and who went. The committees also dictated crops and methods, so that farms 'produced in the best interest of the country'.

The need was so great the experts proposed farming the hillsides, a move that showed the desperation of the situation.

"We need food from the hills," one farming expert said.

A Glimmer in the Dark

The bombings and the attacks continued, on London and other British cities. Coventry, with its automobile and tire factories, that also made aircraft and tanks was devastated in a raid that leveled the center of the city. The great cathedral was destroyed and the ruins left as a symbol of the ugliness of war. The whole nation wept for Coventry.

Bristol, maker of airplanes, was hit. Birmingham, the great industrial city was a target, as was Manchester, the world's first great industrial city. Liverpool, with its miles of docks, was a prime target. Sheffield, maker of steel, was not spared. Glasgow in Scotland, home to great shipyards, suffered attacks.

Hull, a port on the east coast, was frequently hit because it was in the path of returning bombers that still had bombs they hadn't dropped. Belfast, the shipbuilding city in Northern Ireland, took a huge hit on the vast facilities that built warships and military aircraft. The port of Southampton, and the naval bases of Portsmouth and Plymouth were pounded. These were also planned targets of the invasion forces eager to seize ports.

But London was the prize. It was hanging on despite the pounding. What's more, the RAF was still meeting and often defeating the waves of German planes. The factories were replacing the downed planes, and the training schools were replacing the pilots.

The time was past, but remained a state secret, when there were no planes in reserve to send up to fight. That had meant the country was on the verge of losing control of the airspace. The tank was empty. Now it was filling up. More planes rose up to meet the enemy. Still, 'hanging on' was a poor substitute for victory.

It seemed true now what Churchill had said after the Dunkirk evacuation: "May it not be that this civilization itself will be defended by the skill and devotion of a few thousand airmen." Hitler had no idea that the British were straining to hold on.

"The constant alert for invasion imposes a heavy strain on all concerned," Churchill told Parliament.

A big part of that strain, he said, was keeping together 'the body and soul of London's eight million souls' who were surviving 'under artificial conditions of civilization'.

He ordered that British bombers continue to pound German ships, barges, ports, and troop assembly points.

Bad Day in Berlin

In Berlin the reality was sinking in. The invasion plan required air superiority. Without that the Royal Navy could not be bottled up or kept away from the landing beaches.

Some of the top Nazis and leading commanders were having doubts. One of the Wehrmacht commanders said that an invasion with the Royal Navy still in position would be like 'putting our troops through a meat grinder'.

Admiral Raeder, head of the German Navy, and responsible for landing the invasion force, believed the British would go 'all in' to defend their home island 'to the last ship and last man'. He thought this desperation jeopardized the chance of a successful invasion.

Air Force Chief Göring, whose squadrons could not get control of the air over Britain, was losing any enthusiasm for an invasion. Hitler agreed to put the invasion plan on hold. It could always be revived. Hitler began to turn his thoughts to another invasion plan: *Operation Barbarossa*—the invasion of Soviet Russia.

In the meantime the bombing attacks would continue. It made sense to knock out British war-making capacity, and keep it bottled up on its island. The blockade, and the submarine warfare—the Battle of the Atlantic—would continue. Any ship headed for Britain was ripe for sinking.

German forces were also fighting British and Commonwealth forces across North Africa, the Mediterranean, and the Middle East.

All these moves would turn out to be questionable from a German standpoint: failure to knock out the RAF; failure to deal with the Royal Navy; and failure to bomb or starve the country into submission. The decision to open another war front against the Soviet Union would prove to be a strategic catastrophe.

Unconquered Britain would be a platform for the deadly bombing campaign by Britain and the U.S. against Germany. It would be the staging base for the great D-Day invasion of Normandy, France, and conquered Europe.

A war games analysis done in the 1970s indicates the invasion would have failed. German forces would have gained a foothold, and then pushed inland. They would have been slowed at the Stop Lines. Then a powerful counterattack by the heavy elite divisions of the British Army, held in reserve, would have pushed the invaders back. British warships would have swept into the English Channel and the landing zones and cut off supplies and re-enforcements. At that point the invasion fails.

Chapter 3
Smiles Among the Ruins

A Breather from the Blitz

As days and weeks passed with no invasion, Londoners began to breathe a little easily.

The West End, the Theater District, the Piccadilly Circus, the Leicester Square, and the Haymarket hustled and bustled. Movie theaters and stage theaters advertised with huge billboards and marquees. Many films were from Hollywood.

While there were few cars, the red double-decker route-master buses were everywhere, along with trucks and plenty of military vehicles, and motorcycle messengers.

There were concerts with orchestras and bands; solo artists; vaudevillians, such as *Flanagan and Allen*; and concert pianists. These were held at churches, halls, and public spaces around the city.

Radio took people's minds off the war, with BBC entertainment, music and light programs. One program became a national obsession. *It's That Man Again*, known simply as ITMA, gained an audience of 20 million, or 40% of the population. It's credited with bolstering morale.

Comic Tommy Handley plays a fast-talking character who takes various jobs: Minister of Aggravation; mayor of the seaside resort, foaming at the mouth, and many more. He deals with all sorts of odd characters, Mrs. Mopp, Colonel Chinstrap, Mona Lott, Sophie Tuckshop, and a German spy, Funf.

It was famous in part for its fast pace and timeliness, with war-related jokes. *It's That Man Again* actually referred to Hitler and the fact he always popped up in the news as 'that man'. The Royal Family let it be known they were faithful listeners.

The show, heard throughout the war, provided various catchphrases popular in those years: 'This is Funf speaking',

‘Can I do you now, sir?’, ‘Ta ta for now TTFN’, and ‘Don’t mind if I do’.

When creator Tommy Handley died suddenly, thousands lined the streets to the crematorium. Memorial services were held at St. Paul’s and at the Liverpool Cathedral, in his home town. The Bishop of London said, “People had found in his program an escape from their troubles and anxieties.”

Killing Television

People tuned into radio during the war, for news and entertainment, music, dance bands, and talk programs. The war killed—delayed—television for a decade. When war broke out, the BBC was broadcasting television programs in London from a station at Alexandra Palace, an entertainment complex in north London. The BBC published a regular TV schedule in its magazine, *Radio Times*.

War and the need for electronics for air planes, radar, and all sorts of military uses put television on hold. The same thing happened in the U.S. and Germany.

The station was also shut down out of fear that the signals could be used as a homing device by enemy planes. The antenna was used to jam German bomber navigation.

Soothing the Savagery

Music helped soothe the hurts of war. They city’s concert halls and music venues tried to stay open, even though the air raid sirens competed with the performances. Recorded music was the alternative. Across town the Abbey Road recording studios, with its main studio, Studio 1, capable of holding a symphony orchestra, kept turning out recordings.

Americans Glenn Miller and Dinah Shore recorded here during the war. Opera singer Richard Tauber recorded hundreds of songs. Many other artists recorded here: Vladimir Horowitz, violinist Yehudi Menhuin, composer Igor Stravinsky, and cellist Pablo Casals. In 1943, composer Ralph Vaughn Williams debuted his 5th Symphony here, with the London Symphony Orchestra conducted by Sir John Barbirolli.

London’s orchestras stayed busy in the Blitz. These included the London Symphony Orchestra, the London Philharmonic, the BBC Symphony, and the BBC Variety Orchestra. The orchestral conductors were in demand: Barbirolli, Malcolm Sargent, Thomas Beecham, and Adrian Boult.

The Blitz bombing was not kind to the city's theaters and concert halls. People flocked to the theaters and music events, even with the constant threat of bombing.

On May 10, 1941 the London Philharmonic and the Royal Choral Society under the direction of Malcolm Sargent performed the works of Sir Edward W. Elgar, *Enigma Variations* and *A Dream of Gerontius*. The concert was held at *Queen's Hall*, the leading concert hall, a London version of New York's Carnegie Hall. *Queen's* with 2,500 seats was home to the famous Proms—the informal concert series aimed at ordinary folks.

That night, as in so many nights, the bombers came. An incendiary bomb penetrated the main hall. It was gutted, ruined beyond repair. That same night the Houses of Parliament, Westminster Abbey, and the British Museum were also hit.

Luckily, the backup concert hall, *Royal Albert Hall* with 5,000 seats, took over the concerts, including The Proms. The *Royal Opera House* at Covent Garden was turned into a dance hall during the war. *Sadler's Wells Opera Theater* went dark. It was taken over by the government to house people bombed out of their houses. Culture was important, but a place to live was even more important.

The dozens of theaters of the West End tried to stay open, but not all evaded the falling bombs. The *Old Vic Theater*, one of the city's best known, was bombed out in the Blitz. Late in the war it was revived by actors Ralph Richardson and Laurence Olivier.

The *London Coliseum*, one of the biggest music halls, and capable of handling orchestras and ballet, was used for light musicals instead.

The *Savoy*, famous for Gilbert and Sullivan musical comedies, housed a new 1941 comedy play by Noel Coward, *Blithe Spirit*, which would play for 2,000 performances. *Theatre Royal Haymarket* in the war presented plays by Noel Coward, and a number of productions directed or performed by John Gielgud, Hamlet, a Midsummer Night's Dream, and the Beggar's Opera.

Prince of Wales Theater, with 1,100 seats, presented musicals, and in 1941 screened Charlie Chaplin's devastating film mocking Hitler, *The Great Dictator*. Audiences loved it.

The *Palladium*, one of the biggest with 2,300 seats, was used for revues and big events. In 1941, a German parachute bomb, weighing 2,000 pounds and with a clockwork delayed fuse, crashed into the theater. It didn't explode. The Royal Navy bomb squad, in a gut-wrenching exercise, defused the bomb and removed it from the theater. The *Queen's Theater* in Shaftesbury Avenue was not so lucky. Bombs took it out.

London Casino, a big cabaret theater showing musical revues, was severely damaged by the bombing. *Drury Lane Theater*, one of the best known, closed and was taken over by ENSA, the entertainment agency for the armed forces, as its headquarters.

'We Never Closed'

London was no match for the exotic and erotic musical revues and shows of Paris, the Lido and the Folies-Bergère. But it did try. *The Windmill Theatre* on Great Windmill Street off Piccadilly Circus featured nude dancers in elaborate revues. At a time when stage nudity was a no-no, it got past the law by persuading the judges that grand 'living tableaux' with no bodily movement was art and not erotica. The dancers appeared in Greek temples, as living fountains, in historical reproductions. The conceit was, 'If it's got some class, you can show tits and ass.' The Windmill stayed open throughout the war, the Blitz, and the rocket attacks, and used that fact as its slogan, 'We Never Closed.'

It wasn't always easy to keep going. In heavy bombing raids the dancers, variety acts, and musicians headed for the well-protected basement. The shows were popular and ran almost continuously, with the room packed with soldiers and celebrities.

There were some laughs and life went on. But fear of bombs, rationing, mixed news from the war fronts, and worry about loved ones 'out there' in unnamed bases, unmentioned ships, made life hard on the home front.

Chapter 4
The Great March to the East

In June, 1941, the news came that Hitler had turned his wrath, and his armies, against his arch enemy, Stalin and the Soviet Union.

It was to be the greatest invasion in history, with three great fronts moving forward, involving 3 million troops. Hitler must have been aware of what had happened to Napoleon. It was said that Napoleon invaded Russia with 600,000 men and 300,000 horses, and retreated with 30,000 men and no horses.

The Germans enjoyed great early success. Again, the Blitz warfare of rapid movement and encirclement, with massive air attacks and bombing, proved to be unstoppable. The Soviets suffered huge losses.

But the Soviet Union had thousands of miles of territory that permitted retreat and regrouping time and again. Here was a vast nation of 200 million people with seemingly endless resources of manpower and raw materials. The Soviets could move beyond the range of bombers, set up new factories, recruit from the far-flung nationalities of central Asia, and prepare a massive counterattack. The Russian winter would be the greatest ally. It could bring the armored divisions to a halt and make survival—not conquest—the chief priority.

As the Soviets suffered, took huge losses, yet fought on in front of Leningrad, Moscow, and Stalingrad a great wave of sympathy swept over London and Britain.

There had long been a reservoir of support for the ideals of Communism—equality, triumph of the working class—in parts of the British society including some labor unions and among intellectuals, particularly at Cambridge University.

Stafford Cripps, ambassador to the Soviet Union, was greatly moved by what he saw in Moscow. He returned to

London and made radio broadcasts on the BBC about the Soviet resistance to invasion. These were so well received that Cripps saw his political star rise.

The Soviet intelligence agencies took full advantage of this pro-Soviet sentiment to recruit some of the most successful spies in history. The Soviets penetrated the British program set up to build an atom bomb, code named *Tube Alloys*. They had spies in the Foreign Office, the intelligence services, the military, and in embassies, including the British embassy in Washington. They had two British spies in top level science jobs in the Manhattan Project, the American atom bomb project. As the war raged British atom spy Klaus Fuchs came down regularly from Birmingham to London to meet with his Soviet contact and to pass on atomic secrets.

As the weeks and months went on it became increasingly clear that no invasion was imminent. Even so the military chiefs deemed it prudent to keep major forces at the ready in case the invasion threat returned. Intelligence estimates indicated the Germans could muster huge invasion forces and thousands of planes—much more than in Operation Sea Lion—if they thought an all-out knockout punch should be aimed at Britain.

At the end of 1941 the whole war equation changed again. Britain found itself at war with the Empire of Japan, with Japanese forces attacking British colonies, possessions and military bases, including the great naval base at Singapore and the port city of Hong Kong.

Only now Britain had the great ally she needed: the United States. Japan attacked the U.S. at Pearl Harbor and in the Philippines. The U.S. declared war on Japan. Its ally, Germany, declared war on the U.S. Now the war was raging everywhere. The great industrial power of the U.S., and its military and naval resources would raise the prospects of the allied nations.

There were still shocks to come. In a great intelligence failure, the British suffered one of their greatest defeats of all time at Singapore at the hands of a numerically inferior Japanese force.

Now, with the Americans in the war, supplies, weapons, and troops poured to the war fronts. American troops arrived in Britain. A huge buildup began that would lead to an invasion of

French North Africa, then Italy, and finally the great push into Europe at Normandy.

The Americans relieved British troops occupying Iceland. The British had seized the island nation after Germany occupied Denmark and Norway. Some 25,000 British troops were withdrawn.

Hitler's failure to invade and conquer Britain let the island become a super base for armies, ships, and air forces. The RAF and the American Eighth Air Force flew devastating air raids over Germany.

Americans became familiar sights on the streets of London. They brought energy, optimism, lots of chewing gum, and the real hope of victory. Now Germany and Italy began to suffer defeats on all fronts; in the Soviet Union at Stalingrad, in North Africa, then Sicily, and the Italian mainland. Italy faltered, then switched sides to the Allies.

But London was not off the hook. In fact, a nastier hook remained.

Chapter 5
Blitz II: Death from Space

In 1944, the Allies invaded Hitler's Fortress Europe, established a beachhead, and fought toward Paris, the Rhine, and Germany itself.

Hitler fought back with new secret weapons. These weapons would open a new chapter in human history, the birth of advanced rocketry and missiles, and the beginning of the space age.

The first weapon, the V-1 missile was a pilotless flying bomb, somewhat akin to the modern cruise missile. It was a terror weapon because it could not pinpoint a target. The second weapon, the V-2 rocket was the genuine beginning of the space age. It was somewhat more accurate but it too was a terror weapon. It also pushed rocket science forward in one great leap. The V-2:

- Obtained supersonic speeds—3,000 miles per hour.
- Was the first man-made object to reach space about 68 miles up.
- Had a guidance system with a simple analog computer. Some were even radio controlled.
- Was the rocket that was the model for the American Redstone rockets that put the first American, Alan Shepherd, in space.

Werhner Von Braun, science director of the German rocket program, and a hundred other scientists from that program, would be brought to the U.S. after the war. Von Braun would go on to head the Redstone Arsenal, then the Marshall Space Flight

Center in Huntsville, Alabama. He would then build the Saturn Rockets that went to the moon.

In 1944, his goal was to produce rockets to smash London into little pieces. The V-1 and V-2, called Vengeance weapons, rained death on London for months. Hitler ordered they be targeted to London. The other V-2 target, Antwerp, Belgium, was the port used by Allied troops pushing the Germans back across Europe.

The first V-1 hit near a railroad bridge at Mile End, London, on June 13, 1944. It killed eight civilians. Thousands more would be fired, and 2,400 would hit London, killing 6,200 people and wounding 18,000. Almost 8,000 didn't make it to the target.

The V-1 was nicknamed the buzz bomb or the doodlebug. Its pulse jet engine buzzed when it flew. At a programmed point it went into a steep dive, then the engine cut out. It dived to the target with nearly 2,000 pounds of explosives. People could hear it coming. Then silence. Then a terrible explosion. No one knew where it would fall.

Sunday in the Chapel

One of the worst incidents happened on a Sunday morning in June, 1944. Hundreds of Guardsmen of the Royal Household Division, and family members, were at the regular religious service at the Guards Chapel near Buckingham Palace. The organ played, hymns were sung. The Bishop of Maidstone was presiding at the altar. Suddenly, the attendees heard a distant buzzing. It grew louder and became a roar. Then the sound stopped—the engine cut out.

Then, silence. The V-1 rocket dived into the chapel roof with its deadly warhead. The explosion collapsed the roof which fell on the soldiers and civilians below. The attack killed 121 people and injured 141.

The news of the blast was at first kept secret. Why let the enemy know their success? Why let them know the rocket settings had put it near the palace? Word got out anyway. The chapel was left a roofless ruin for years, and then rebuilt. The bishop was one of the few people not killed or injured. The altar was covered by an arch that did not collapse.

The V-1s had a weak spot—they flew no faster than an airplane, about 370 miles per hour. The V-2 rockets were a different story. They were launched straight up to the edge of space—60 miles or more. Then they dived in an arc to the target area at supersonic speeds.

They broke the sound barrier—CRACK, CRACK—then hit the ground with 2,000 pounds of explosives. They were unstoppable and seemed to come from nowhere.

On September 8, 1944, Duncan Sandys, a member of the war cabinet, was on a London street. He heard that CRACK, CRACK sound and commented to his companion, "That's a rocket!"

In West London, the first V-2 rocket hit a residential district. The blast of 1,600 pounds of Amatol explosives leveled 11 houses and severely damaged 15, with blast damage to 516 houses. Remarkably, only 3 people were killed. Attempts to report the event were blocked by media censors. The official story said 'a gas main exploded.'

Of course, censorship didn't last long. It didn't take long for the public to realize they were under rocket attack. The Germans publicized the attacks. Thousands of V-1s and V-2s were targeted at London. Just as in the Blitz bombing of 1940-41, these new terror assaults provoked a mixture of fear, resignation, and resistance.

Again, children were evacuated in trains dubbed, 'Doodlebug Expresses' after the nickname for the V-1s.

A special committee was convened to try to devise ways to block or minimize the attacks. A series of strategies were developed, particularly against the more vulnerable V-1s.

Because they flew low—3,000 feet—and at airplane speed they could be shot down using fighter planes and anti-aircraft guns. Another tactic was to bomb the launch sites across the English Channel. A gauntlet of anti-aircraft guns was placed between the Channel and London, covering the main launch route. Spotters looked for the rockets then phoned details to area command posts that could then scramble fighter planes or alert the ground gunners. 2,000 barrage balloons hung over London, with the tethering cables acting as a further protection.

A couple of types of fighter planes were capable of chasing down the buzz bombs and then shooting them down. At first a lot of the rockets got through but interception got better. Planes didn't even have to shoot down the rockets. In a daring maneuver they could use a wing to 'tip' the rocket off-course and make it crash in open country.

Simple analog computers, radars, new guns, and sights helped turn the tide. One newsreel narrator referred to the 'almost supernatural struggle between the weapons of science and their robot adversaries.' The defenses became so effective that on August 28, 1944, of 97 V-1s fired at London, 90 were shot down.

Firing airplane machine guns and cannons at the missile had its own dangers because the V-1 carried a 2,000 pound bomb that could take down a plane.

The First Jet Plane

In 1944, British plane-makers, led by Frank Whittle, produced a jet fighter plane. The first jet plane. This was the *Meteor*. It could fly around 500 miles per hour, or more than 150 miles an hour faster than propeller-driven planes. Enough planes were produced to create a squadron of a dozen or more planes. The Germans and Americans were also working on jets and would produce them.

The German jet flew but was never really used in the war. The British found an immediate role for the *Meteor*, the first combat mission for a jet: chase down and destroy the V-1 missiles. It was the perfect role because it kept the planes over British territory and out of German hands. In all, the defenses shot down or stopped several thousand V-1s.

Stopping a V-2 was far harder. Here was a rocket that weighed 14 tons and stood 46 feet tall. It was fueled by 8 tons of alcohol and liquid oxygen, it reached outer space, and flew at 3,000 miles per hour. It had a guidance system with an analog computer and a deadly 2,000-pound warhead. It cost $3.5 million to build one—6,000 were built by concentration camp inmates. "We have invaded space with our rocket," said General Walter Dornberger who set up the rocket program.

But the V-2 also invaded a lot of spaces in London with devastating effects. A V-2 slammed into a Woolworth department store killing 160 people. Another V-2 that fell in Whitechapel, London, killed 130. In late 1944, a V-2 hit the Rex Cinema in Antwerp, killing 567 people.

One tactic used to lessen damage was to put out false reports about where the rockets landed. This information, crucial to calibrating and programming the rockets, was picked up by the Germans. They then mistakenly changing the settings on the rockets.

This had drawbacks because the Germans were double-checking to find out where rockets had hit. They had a handful of agents in London, and they also monitored media reports. Since the British had broken the German codes they knew whether the Germans knew they were being fed false information.

The rocket campaign, which lasted about 10 months, caused 22,000 casualties, including 6,500 dead, and destroyed or damaged 1,127,000 buildings and houses.

The Blitz bombing of 1940-41 caused 92,000 casualties and destroyed or damaged 1,150,000 buildings and houses.

Failed Terror

How effective were the rocket attacks? Most analysts agree they had no impact on the outcome of the war. London was not devastated and abandoned. The government didn't sue for peace. There was no demoralization or mass panic. Terror didn't work.

The conventional bombing by the Americans and the RAF blasted and burned down German cities. That strategy has also been criticized as excessive and not needed because the war was essentially won.

Still, the drive to develop more terrible weapons was relentless. The British were not going to be outdone. At the end of the war they unveiled the Grand Slam, a monstrous 22,000 pound bomb, perhaps the largest conventional weapon up to that time. It could take out almost any structure. The British dropped 42 of them on Germany, on hardened targets such as submarine docking pens.

Chapter 6
War and Revolution: Birth of the Welfare State

In the middle of the Blitz bombing of London, Alexander Fleming was working on penicillin, the first antibiotic; poet T. S. Eliot, with helmet and boots, was helping people to the shelters as an Air Raid Warden. Economist John Maynard Keynes was at the Bank of England struggling with the finances of fighting a World War. In the Westminster district a senior British civil servant was working on a report that would change the world of work, school, and medical care. Sir William Beveridge was putting together a 300-page document that reflected the work of a government super committee of ministries dealing with health, taxes, the treasury, home affairs, and worker compensation.

The war with its death, destruction, and even an =existential threat spurred the leaders of the major parties to look ahead to the future after the war—if there was a future. Conservatives and the left-wing Labor party governed in a coalition. Deputy Prime Minister Clement Atlee, who also headed the Labor Party, pushed for a report on how to improve social conditions, health care, and the general condition of the population.

In a nation totally mobilized with everyone involved in the war it was clear something was amiss. There was too much poverty and bad housing. By some estimates a third of the nation was poorly housed and in poor health. Yet Britain had to win a war, rebuild its ruined cities, and revive its industries to export goods. 'Export or die' would be the slogan. There had to be changes.

"War is a revolutionary moment in world history," Beveridge said. "It's not a time for patching things."

Maybe it was time for revolutionary change. The government had already begun to act. In 1940, the Food Policy Committee, chaired by Atlee, distributed free milk to mothers and children and expanded school lunches. Local governments were offering subsidized meals. Food subsidies of all kinds amounted to $800 million in 1941 dollars.

The German bombing campaign was accomplishing slum clearance in East London. New housing—better housing—would have to be built. The evacuation of children from the cities had also revealed poor health conditions. Military medical exams made similar revelations. A lot of men weren't fit to fight. In 1942, the report was issued by the government. It had a less than snappy title:

SOCIAL INSURANCE AND ALLIED SERVICES
By Sir William Beveridge
York House, Kingsway, London W. C.2

The title was dull, the impact was earth-shattering. The report marked the birth of the Welfare State, socialized medicine, and 'cradle to grave' social services.

In hundreds of pages of bureaucratic language the report proposed ways to improve the lot of millions of people and create a 'minimum level' of social protection—a safety net for everyone. That would include universal health care. The stated aims were to combat poor health, poverty, bad housing, inadequate education, and unemployment. The Big Five.

The public liked the report. Opinion polling showed widespread support. Labor, the left and worker groups lent support. Leaders of the major political parties praised the effort, including Conservatives. Church leaders called it a manifestation of the Christian ethic. The Archbishop of Canterbury, William Temple, argued for social reform and championed a kind of 'Christian Socialism', which he promoted in a popular book.

Prime Minister Churchill did not dispute the need. He even used the term 'cradle to grave' coverage. He never rejected the basic idea. He did have reservations about the cost, the size, scope, and timing. How would it be financed in the middle of a war with billions of pounds of debt piling up? There was even some dissent within the Labor Party. The Earl of Glasgow worried that the nation 'will owe more money than any country in the world'. He added that Britain would become a major debtor nation.

The war was costing $60 million a day in 1940 dollars, the national debt was expected to grow to $100 billion. Records showed that tax and government revenues only met 52% of the budget; the balance came from borrowing. Estimates showed that new social welfare spending increases and debt servicing could add $5 billion to expenditures.

That was the pessimistic view. There was a far more optimistic view. The country could pay for a welfare state based on peace and prosperity, the kind of productivity increases seen in the United States, plus full employment, good exports, and high economic growth. On top of that would be huge savings from better health, a better work force, less illnesses and absenteeism, and more production. The end result: a win for everyone.

One big debate in the middle of the war was over the rise in venereal disease and whether the government should require mandatory tracing of partners and treatment. There were thousands of cases. Some blamed 'foreigners', sailors, soldiers, prostitutes, and war in general. A health official quoted Shakespeare: "Lechery, lechery, still, war and lechery."

Lady Astor said in Parliament that war conditions, alcohol, loneliness, and moral laxness caused the problem, along with men chasing naïve girls. She called for more education, women doctors, and women police to counsel younger women. Just about everyone agreed the rise of VD was one more health problem that hurt production, fostered absenteeism, and in the words of one woman Member of Parliament 'did more damage than Nazi airplanes'.

J. B. Priestly, the author and playwright who gave popular talks on the BBC, warned that the war would change everything and the country would not go back to business as usual after the war. The influx of women into the workplace and the military, the changing mores, and now the Beveridge report were mounting proof that he was right.

First the war had to be won. Then the great changes could take place. The war was won, and change did come. First the electorate, tired of war and deprivation, voted Churchill and the Conservatives out of power. They lauded his wartime leadership, but for peacetime they longed for change.

Labor's Clement Atlee was voted in as the new prime minister in 1945. He began to implement much of the Beveridge plan with passage of a series of laws, including the National Health Service Act that created universal free health care paid for by social insurance fees and taxes. This was the controversial 'socialized medicine' that is still argued about today but that is supported by all the political parties.

Other laws dealt with housing, re-construction, and unemployment. Atlee and his party went on to nationalize major industries, including the big four railroads, devastated by the war. The state enterprise became British Railways. Steel and other industries got similar take-overs. The government now ran vast enterprises with millions of employees. The labor unions wielded vast power. Wartime austerity and rationing would continue. Imports far exceeded exports and the trade imbalance grew.

The 'victorious' British struggled to compete in a world where the United States emerged from war richer, stronger, and a dominant power in a wrecked world.

Atlee was also eager to get out of the 'Empire business', and 400 million people of India were given their independence.

As time went on, it became clear that 'socialized' or state-directed enterprises were a poor and inefficient way to compete in the world. In coming decades many industries were again privatized.

The welfare state programs and the National Health system remained in place. The question became how to produce enough wealth to pay for the generous benefits. That called for innovation, private investment, efficiency and productivity, and some degree of cooperation between labor and management.

The search for that right balance between state control and private enterprise continues to this day. At the same time no major political party is calling for elimination or major dismantling of the welfare state.

Chapter 7
War Movies

Hollywood on the Thames

Films would play a major role in the war effort. Even as the bombs fell, film production continued at the dozen or so film studios scattered around the western and southern London suburbs.

Production shifted to films that would help the war effort, boost morale, train soldiers and civil defense workers, or highlight the heroism of soldiers, sailors, firemen, air raid workers, and even ordinary citizens.

The filmmakers would turn their skills to propaganda films, which they often made with great skill that transcended mere propaganda. Call it well-made propaganda for a good cause. The Ministry of Information, the Crown Film Unit, the Colonial Film Unit, and production units of the Navy, Army, and Royal Air Force cranked out films aimed at helping the war effort.

At one point the spokesman for the Ministry of Information told Parliament that the ministry was making films in 14 movie studios across the country. He was asked whether he was worried about the content of British films.

"We make films of a propaganda nature," he explained. In one fiscal year, 1943-44, some 160 films and newsreels were cranked out by the ministry, which also gave assistance to commercial filmmakers.

At the same time the private studios continued to make lighter fare, silly comedies, dramas, and even a musical or two. Even these films often had war themes about newly drafted soldiers, including women, faced with the rigors and dangers of military life.

In *King Arthur was a Gentleman*, a musical comedy made at Gaumont British Studios, an inept civilian with a fascination for King Arthur is drafted into an Army mechanized regiment. His mates plant an old sword in the barracks and make the protagonist believe it's King Arthur's sword. The ruse pays off when the draftee and his fellow soldiers, including women of the Army Territorial Service, defeat the Nazis in North Africa—with King Arthur's help. All this is accompanied by a dozen song and dance numbers.

This was typical of the lighter fare, but far more serious films came off the production line. The largest studio, Denham Studios/ London Films, was new, an art-deco complex built by Hungarian refugee and filmmaker, Alexander Korda. The studio produced some of the best films in the war, including the much- honored *In Which We Serve*, about the life and death of a British destroyer at war in the high seas. Famed actor and writer Noel Coward played the ship's captain who turns the crew into a fighting force. We also learn about the private lives of the crew and their families, played by leading film actors, Richard Attenborough, John Mills, Celia Johnson, and Michael Wilding.

Coward, film director David Lean, and cinematographer Ronald Neame would go on to make other highly praised films. What made the film rise above most war films was the fact that the destroyer, the heroic fighting ship, was attacked and sunk. It was controversial to show the defeat and loss of a ship in the midst of a war. The film was nominated for two Academy Awards, including best picture of 1942.

Denham Studios also made several award-winning Technicolor films during the war, at a time when color films meant added expense and technical input.

On the eve of the 1944, Normandy invasion of France, actor-director Laurence Olivier released his adaption of Shakespeare's *Henry V* about a king who invaded France. Here was an epic film requiring thousands of extras to recreate the battle of Agincourt. Prime Minister Winston Churchill pushed for the film to be completed as a morale-booster.

On the eve of battle, Olivier delivered the famous St. Crispin's Day speech: "We few, we happy few, we band of brothers…"

The film is famous for its tracking shot of the French knights, in full armor, riding full tilt toward the English lines. Extras were offered extra money if they could bring their own horses. The film is also memorable for its use of sets designed to look like medieval paintings. These sets give the movie a kind of storybook quality.

Henry V won four Academy Awards and was nominated as best picture. American critic James Agee called the film, 'One of cinema's great works of art.'

Another color epic film won many honors. The movie-making team of Michael Powell and Eric Pressburger, known as the *Archers*, released, *The Life and Death of Colonel Blimp*, which documented British-German relations over a half century as embodied by a British Army officer and a German officer. The film follows the two officers from the turn of the century to World War II. The Germans are shown as stiff-necked, rigid, and militaristic. The British are portrayed as reasonable ladies and gentlemen interested in peaceful co-existence. The film shifts in time, with numerous flashbacks as Britain prepares for possible invasion in 1940. The protagonist General Kandy returns from retirement to become commander of the new Home Guard. He reconciles with the German officer who is now in Britain. In the last scene, General Kandy and the soldiers who look up to him are preparing for the battles to come. London and the country will be defended.

"They are coming into the city now, the army, with bands," he is told. There is the sense that British pluck and resolve will win the day and that 'right makes might'.

One of the grandest films, a Technicolor epic, *The Four Feathers*, was made in 1939 just before the outbreak of war. It's a tale of cowardice and courage set in Egypt and Sudan as a British Army advances into Sudan against a rebellious tribal army. One British officer refuses to serve, resigns, and is insulted by his fellow officers who send him white feathers—a sign of cowardice. To redeem himself he goes to Egypt, disguises himself as a mute tribal member, and tries to rejoin his regiment. With acts of courage he reconciles with his fellow soldiers and his future bride.

The film, shot in the Sudan, has one of the great set pieces in movies. The Army's flotilla of boats and a gunboat struggle up the Fifth Cataract of the Nile, pulled from shore with cables by hundreds of native workers who chant as they pull. The sweeping scene was shot at the Nile Cataract without special effects. Zoltan Korda directed the film, shot in part at Denham Studios by London Films.

Ealing Studios, a prestigious label, issued the classic film about an imagined German occupation of Britain, *Went the Day Well*? In the film ordinary British citizens, men and women, fight back against a brutal enemy. Ealing also released comedies and the spooky thriller, *Dead of Night*.

Pinewood Studios was taken over by the government and used by the Crown Film Unit, the Army, the Royal Air Force and the Polish Air Force in exile to make award-winning patriotic documentaries, including *Desert Victory, Coastal Command,* and *Western Approaches* about the deadly anti-submarine warfare in the Atlantic.

Some of the documentaries were aimed as much for overseas consumption as for domestic use. The British wanted to influence the Americans and build sympathy for Britain's plight; and bolster support in Canada, which had sent troops and aid to the 'mother country'. One film, *London can Take It*, exemplified these films. Narrated by a Canadian journalist, the film showed a city under relentless attack from the air by day and night. Still, the city fought back, with anti-aircraft guns, searchlights, and barrage balloons to stop any low-level attacks. The air-raid wardens and Fire Brigade dealt with the hundreds, and even thousands, of fires and explosions. Each morning the city picks itself up and goes back to work, as millions pick their way through the bombed-out ruins.

Humphrey Jennings, a skilled filmmaker, produced a number of highly praised 'propaganda' short films. None was more lauded than *Listen to Britain*, which rose above mere documentary and soft propaganda to the level of poetry and art. The film has no narration. The people speak for themselves in their daily and nightly activities. Children play in the playground and chant a childhood ditty; miners plunge deep into the earth. Women of the Women's Land Army march into the fields for the harvest. Vaudeville comics do their routine for a largely uniformed audience. Women in arms factories labor while the radio plays 'music to work by'.

In the famous ballroom scene, hundreds of couples dance as a band plays, *Roll out the barrel*. The dancers move together in a swirling counterclockwise mass. Workers attend a noon-time Air Force band concert in Central London. The Queen sits with them. Excerpts from this film, un-credited, have appeared in countless TV and cable documentaries about the war period.

(Now this film and many others are available on YouTube or the Internet.)

In most cases, the documentary cameramen rode on the planes, the ships, the submarines, and the tanks in combat. In *Target for Tonight* the cameras followed the Bomber Command planes from the beginning of a raid over Germany to its conclusion. Spy planes returned with photos of targets, the pilots and crews are briefed, the planes take off and face death flying to and returning from targets.

Some films combined documentary style with theatrical narrative, as in *One of Our Aircraft is Missing*, about a British plane shot down over Germany and Holland. The crew escapes through Holland and is helped by the Dutch people. This was another Powell—Pressburger film (The Archers). To make scenes seem real, an exact full-scale replica of the Wellington bomber was built in the Riverside Studio. Lights, special effects, simulated explosions, and smoke made viewers think they were on a bombing run. The film was nominated for two Academy Awards. Humphrey Jennings' film *Fires were Started* combined 143 real actors, amateur actors, and a documentary style to document the desperate work of London's Fire Brigade in the 1940-41 Blitz bombing. The Crown Film Unit filmed interiors at Pinewood Studios, but exteriors were filmed in the London streets. The film is on several lists of the Hundred Best British Films.

Gainsborough Studios produced a trio of films featuring women in the war. In *Millions Like Us*, women are shown leaving their easy civilian life for the rigors of war production, in this case an aircraft factory. In *Two Thousand Women* the story centers on an internment camp set up in France to hold British women. In *Waterloo Road*, a soldier goes AWOL to save his wife from the advances of a shady character back home.

The British wanted and needed Americans in the war. They wanted to show the ties between the two countries. No film did that more than *A Canterbury Tale* made in 1944 on the eve of the invasion of Europe. There were hundreds of thousands of American soldiers in Britain.

In the film, an American Army sergeant is making a pilgrimage to Canterbury Cathedral, much in the fashion of the pilgrims in Chaucer's famous *Canterbury Tales*. He meets a British sergeant who played the organ in a London movie theater in peacetime, and a young English woman headed home. They wind up stranded in a quaint village in Kent. They work to find the culprit who has been assaulting women at the train station. The American is intrigued by the people in the village, their strange customs and manners, and their obsession with tea. (The American says he prefers marijuana to tea, an observation ahead of its time.) He meets the 'land girls' on the farms, the Home Guard, the Fire Watchers, and the Air Raid Wardens. The culprit, a local official, confesses to his assaults.

The pilgrims make it to Canterbury, to the cathedral. The British sergeant plays Bach on the great organ. The American learns to like the Brits. The young woman walks the bombed-out streets with the grand cathedral in the background. In the last scene hundreds of soldiers gather at the cathedral, the organist plays *Onward Christian Soldiers*. Everyone joins in the singing.

The film was made by the Powell—Pressburger team under the British Lion label. The U.S. Army cooperated in the making of the picture. It remains perhaps the prime example of Anglo-American propaganda in film—shot in brilliant black and white.

One film worth mentioning, *The Way Ahead* (also called, *Immortal Battalion*), was made by two actors who would have famous film careers: David Niven and Peter Ustinov. Lt. Colonel Niven, a combat Commando who saw action, and Ustinov, a private, worked for the British Army Film Unit. The movie documents British troops fighting Erwin Rommel's *Afrika Korps* in North Africa. Niven already had a career in Hollywood when he rejoined the Army. Ustinov would go on to win two Academy Awards for best supporting actor.

British Gaumont and Pathe Studios produced hundreds of newsreels shown weekly in British theaters. They, too, documented the war in detail with dramatic film shot by combat cameramen. Citizens could duck into movie theaters, including theaters that featured newsreel and see film clips of the Blitz, fighter plane dogfights, and scenes of British triumphs, such as the taking of Addis Ababa, the Ethiopian capital, from the Italians.

The narrator mocks the fighting ability of the Italians, as a regiment of white South African soldiers marches in, drums beating and bagpipes skirling.

One movie studio, Shepperton, went to war in a real sense. It was in the pathway to the Vickers-Armstrong aircraft factory, which was bombed by German planes. Shepperton shut down, was taken over by the government and used to manufacture decoy aircraft and parts for the Vickers Wellington bomber. After the war, Shepperton went on to make many famous films, and its five water tanks became the place to go for underwater filming.

All was not war and destruction in the movies. The studios produced comedies and dramas under a number of company labels: Two Cities, Gainsborough, J. Arthur Rank, British Lion, and the Associated British.

Comics Will Hay, Norman Wisdom, Arthur Askey, Alistair Sim, George Formby, Tommy Handley, and Gracie Fields starred in lightweight comedies, some of them with song and dance. Formby is often described as a British version of Robin Williams. He sang, played the ukulele, and engaged in screwball comedy, with plenty of fast-talking double-entendres delivered in his high-pitched voice.

Tommy Handley's film career was brief, but his fame was massive. He starred in the enormously popular war-time radio comedy, *It's That Man Again*, which drew 20 million listeners—40 % of the population. Handley made the show into a popular movie with the same title.

A lot of the plots of these 'B' movies revolved around the war effort, the military, women in war work, and old guys serving in the Home Guard. Many of the stories end with ordinary Britons beating the Nazis, uncovering a spy ring, or exhibiting courage under fire.

One British 'propaganda' film became world famous for its music. London composer Richard Addinsell was asked to compose a piano concerto for the 1941 film *Dangerous Moonlight* made at the British studio of RKO Radio Pictures. The story follows a Polish pianist and fighter pilot who sees his home city, Warsaw, and his country devastated by Nazi invaders. The pilot eventually escapes to Britain and joins the RAF to fight as a pilot in the Battle of Britain.

Addinsell wrote his *Warsaw Concerto* in a romantic style that imitated Tchaikovsky and Rachmaninoff. The film received lukewarm critical acclaim, but the music was a hit around the world, selling millions of copies. The music is still played as a concert piece.

Mysteries and crime dramas were also popular. They served to take people's minds off the horrors of war.

Women, who were increasingly liberated by the war's need for bodies, workers, and soldiers regardless of gender, got the attention of filmmakers. In a much-honored film, *Brief Encounter*, a middle-class housewife in a boring marriage has a brief romance with a married doctor she meets at a railroad station. The two lovers sense that despite their passion nothing but grief will follow if they continue to see each other. Their children will suffer; their spouses will be deeply wounded. In one of film's weepiest tear-jerking scenes, the lovers part company for the last time at the same train station where they met. The film, directed by David Lean and starring Celia Johnson and Trevor Howard, was based on a one act play by Noel Coward. It was shot on location and at Denham Studios. The film won the Cannes Film Festival in 1946, and received two Academy Award nominations, for best actress and best director.

The film is famous for the use of music. Rachmaninoff's romantic Second Piano Concerto is played throughout the film.

In the film, *I Know Where I'm Going,* a young middle-class go-getter from London, played by Wendy Hiller, is off to the Hebrides Islands of Scotland to marry a rich industrialist who is staying on one of the islands. Bad weather keeps her from crossing to the island. She meets a young naval officer while she is waiting out the storm. They are attracted to one another. It turns out he is the Lord of the Island, the Laird. He tells about the curse of the local castle that involves two lovers who died there, and who put a curse on his family. They try to cross to the island, but nearly die when the boat is trapped in a giant tidal whirlpool. They manage to escape. Back on land, the Laird deliberately triggers the curse by entering the ruined castle. The heroine abandons any idea of marriage, and pursues the Laird—fulfilling the curse that says two lovers will be bound together for eternity. The team of Powell and Pressburger directed the film, which was made at Denham and on location. The whirlpool was re-created in the studio water tank.

American director Martin Scorsese called the film 'a masterpiece'. Representative of the movies that boosted morale, entertained, and provided a needed diversion was a musical film made in 1942 at Riverside Studio by Columbia British. It was no masterpiece, and is largely forgotten, but it served its purpose.

We'll Meet Again starred Vera Lynn, the young singer 'adopted' by the Armed Forces after her title song won the hearts of the nation. In this film she plays herself, with a different name. She comes to London to be a dancer, but people like her voice. In a bomb shelter during an air raid she's persuaded to sing. She's discovered. She teams up with a song writer and they pursue show business success. The highlight is the famous song that became a kind of anthem for the war years: '*We'll meet again, don't know where, don't know when…*'

When America got into the war, American filmmakers got into the act. In Frank Capra's film series, *Why We Fight*, one episode is devoted to the Battle of Britain. In the documentary, *Know Your Ally: Britain*, American actor Walter Huston tries to explain the British to the Americans who now flood into the island nation in preparation to invade Hitler's Fortress Europe.

Another excellent and atmospheric American film, made in 1940, featured the unsung sailors of the British Merchant Marine. They would lose more than 2,000 ships and 32,000 sailors in the struggle to supply Britain. John Ford's *The Long Voyage Home* tells the story of a British merchant ship sailing from the Caribbean with a mixed crew to Baltimore to pick up a dangerous cargo of explosives that then must be taken to Britain through the German blockade of submarines and planes. The captain and the crew from several countries risk their lives and know they will get little in return. Is one of them a spy? Will the good-natured Swede finally make it back to Sweden? Will they survive the crossing?

Ford, a Navy man, tells a story drawn from several short Eugene O'Neill plays. The movie looks at the men who go to sea and take the long voyage that may never get them home. The critic for the *New York Times* said, "The film is one of the most honest pictures ever placed on the screen." It was nominated for six Academy Awards.

Londoners flocked to the movies theaters—the cinema—for a little relief from the unbearable tensions of war. The heart of the movie district, the West End, was Leicester Square, near Soho, and Piccadilly. Here, were large movie 'palaces', including the Empire, Europe's largest movie theater. The newspapers reported any movie theaters destroyed by the bombing.

Many of the war-time filmmakers and actors went on to produce distinguished films in the post-war years in a period that was a golden age of British cinema that ended in the mid-1950s with the rise of television.

Alexander Korda, one of the most prolific British filmmakers, was knighted for his war-time films and became Sir Alexander Korda.

War Movies, Berlin Style

While British filmmakers were creating films that showed Germans as villainous aggressors and Britons as brave adversaries, in Berlin the film industry was cranking out anti-British movies.

The German film industry had once been one of the most vibrant. With the rise of Hitler many directors, producers, and actors escaped to Hollywood, including such stalwarts as Billy Wilder, Fritz Lang, Peter Lorre, Marlene Dietrich, film composers Eric Korngold, and Kurt Weill.

Those who remained were Nazis or were simply unable or unwilling to challenge the new order. In the war years the filmmakers churned out propaganda films, documentaries, comedies, fluffy musicals, and anti-British, anti-Jewish, and anti-Soviet dramas.

Leni Riefensthal won fame with her choreographed documentaries about the Nazi Party rallies and the Olympic Games. These films pioneered new filming and editing techniques. Some stars continued making film in the Third Reich: singer Zarah Leander and actor Emil Jannings. Many film were made at the big UFA studios at Potsdam.

One anti-British film was *Titanic*, about the sinking of the luxury ocean liner on its first voyage. The film portrays its British owners as greedy and unconcerned about the passengers. An anti-British documentary was titled *The English Disease*. The British were the bad guys in a film drama, *Ohm Kruger*, about the Boer War in South Africa.

The documentaries, *Battle for Norway* and *U-Boats Westward,* chronicled German action against the British and French. *The Fox of Glenarvon* is about a fictional Irish county where the residents fight against British rule. Several German films attacked Britain's 'colonialism', even though the Germans resented their loss of the African colonies.

In another bit of irony, at the same time Laurence Olivier was making his big color film, *Henry V,* about a war with France, German filmmakers were filming a color war epic, *Kolberg*, about a German town's resistance to Napoleon's Army. Some 50,000 soldiers served as extras in the filming. Propaganda Minister Goebbels ordered the making of the film to bolster morale. A few days after the film's opening in Berlin the real town of Kolberg fell to the Russians.

The Never-Ending War

World War II has provided seemingly endless material for movies, TV shows, documentaries, books, and dramas. Here was a war with clearly villainous enemies—European fascism, Japanese Imperialism. The moral and ethical lines seemed clearly delineated.

By contrast the cold and hot wars with Communism seemed less clear-cut as to villainy, although Stalin, Mao, Pol Pot, and others killed and imprisoned millions, and struck down any chance of choice or freedom. Their excesses somehow seemed more politically acceptable.

Now a new generation of actors and directors has come along to show how they, too, won World War II. Brad Pitt, George Clooney, Quentin Tarantino, John Travolta, Tom Hanks, Ben Affleck, Stephen Spielberg, and many others have ventured forth to avenge the wrongs, save the stolen art, break the codes, and kill the enemy en masse. And sell plenty of tickets in so doing. The horrors of war become the stuff of plays and screenplays, and plenty of profits.

Chapter 8
War of the Words

London's Feisty Wartime Press

London was, and is, the media and press capital of Britain. A compact and densely populated nation allowed for huge national newspapers that were edited in London but printed and distributed all over the British Isles.

The press would play a crucial role in the war and in the city's sense of itself. The great press center, probably the world's largest concentration of journalism was Fleet Street in Central London. Here were the 'street of ink', the Grub Street and 'ink-stained wretches' of Dr. Samuel Johnson. Here were the great national newspapers, numerous magazines and illustrated journals, news services and thousands of reporters, editors, columnists, and photographers.

The biggest players were the tabloid papers and middle-brow broadsheets with circulations in the millions. These were feisty, brash, and often sensational papers. They championed the average citizen, the Londoners on the subway and the double-decker buses. The editors and reporters were no respecters of the powerful or pretentious. They certainly had low opinions of the dictators Hitler, Mussolini, Stalin, and the Japanese war lords. These papers were also highly political, and were often tied philosophically to the nation's political parties, the Conservatives, the Labor—socialist—party, and others. The Communists had their own paper, *The Daily Worker.*

The Daily Express exemplified these newspapers. With 2.6 million daily copies sold it battled with rivals to be the biggest paper. From its art deco black glass headquarters on Fleet Street it influenced public opinion, voting, and policies promoting war and peace.

Its logo, a Crusader Knight with lance, was one of the most recognized symbols in the country. The powerful owner and publisher, one of the so-called press barons, Lord Beaverbrook, a Canadian, wielded great influence in British government and political circles.

When war came, Churchill chose Beaverbrook to serve in the war cabinet. He was put in charge of the vital aircraft industry. To survive Britain had to produce all the fighters and bombers possible in the shortest possible time. Beaverbrook was given the power to do whatever was needed to build the planes to fight the Nazi air onslaught.

The great rival was the *Daily Mirror*, with 1.4 million daily copies sold. The *Mirror*, with its press baron owner Lord Rothermere had close ties to the Labor Party. Other 'popular' papers included the *Daily Sketch*, a tabloid, and the *Evening Standard*, which would play a role in pushing Britain and Germany toward war. (More on that later.)

On a higher level were the so-called 'quality papers', with their long and erudite features and commentaries, lengthy obituaries, and influential Letters to the Editors. Among these were the *Telegraph*, with its appeal to the establishment Conservatives; and the *Times of London*, 'the Good Grey Lady', the newspaper of record, and probably the country's best known newspaper.

Scattered among the lanes, alleys and squares around Fleet Street were dozens of magazines, illustrated weeklies, and specialized publications of all kinds, including humor magazines such as *Punch.* The illustrated publications, with their photos, illustrations, and artwork covered the great events of a world capital, state visits, Royal occasions, military pageantry, investitures, famous horse races and sporting events, and the comings and goings of celebrities. They chronicled the pomp, circumstance and color of what then was a vast empire. The best known of these, *The Illustrated London News*, invented the genre. Its editor, Bruce Ingram, was the senior editor on Fleet Street, and had been on the job for decades. *ILN* controlled a stable of other publications, including the *Graphic* and the *Tatler*.

The top editors wielded real power. At the top of that list was Geoffrey Dawson of *The Times*. Dawson was a friend of the powerful, particularly Prime Minister Neville Chamberlain, in power at the outbreak of the war, and Lord Halifax, the foreign secretary. Dawson favored a conciliatory stance toward Hitler, a so-called appeasement policy. Both Chamberlain and Halifax famously followed the appeasement route, and were greatly discredited for it. As editor of the nation's most influential newspaper, Dawson encouraged and backed the appeasers. Dawson was also opposed to the creation of a Jewish homeland in Palestine.

The Ultimate Cartoonist

If Dawson wanted to keep Britain out of war at all costs, a newspaperman at another London paper did a lot to get the country into the war. David Low worked as an editorial cartoonist for the *Evening Standard*. He was good at his job. Some believe he was the best political cartoonist ever.

He was certainly effective. His cartoons of the dictators, Hitler, Stalin, and Mussolini, were devastating and drew angry protests from those governments. German propaganda minister, Joseph Goebbels, warned foreign secretary Lord Halifax that Low's cartoons were pushing the two nations toward war. One of the most famous cartoons appeared after Hitler and Stalin signed a so-called non-aggression pact, which would be broken in due time. In the cartoon, Hitler bows and greets Stalin,

"Scum of the earth, I believe?"

Stalin bows and replies, "Bloody assassin of the workers, I presume?"

After the start of the war, Low drew a cartoon showing a lone Englishman on the shore shaking his fist at the waves of German bombers overhead. The caption read: 'All Right. Alone if necessary.' Indeed, at that point, Britain was fighting alone.

The notorious SS Invasion book of British residents to be arrested and eliminated after an invasion contained the name of David Low. Even the crossword puzzles would play a role in the war. The British needed desperately to find people with the skills to decrypt secret codes, such as that used by the German 'Enigma' coding machine. The code-breakers were set up at an estate north of London, Bletchley Park.

One of the chief screening tests for potential code-breakers was to find people who could complete crossword puzzle in *The Telegraph* in less than ten minutes.

Publish and Maybe Perish

The newspapers published even as the bombs fell. There was official censorship, but the newspapers managed to tell the story of the horrors of Blitz warfare and seemingly unending bombing.

There were stories of 'outrages' in the Atlantic, when German submarines attacked ships carrying children evacuated from Britain. In one case, nearly a hundred children drowned.

'Another bomb on Buckingham Palace,' read one headline.

'St. Paul's Saved,' said another, after a blockbuster bomb landed near the landmark cathedral.

A reporter on the south coast reported on the giant German guns in France that were lobbing shells across the English Channel.

'I timed the flash. In a little more than a minute, I head a huge explosion and saw the flames,' the reporter wrote.

In August, 1940, the *Daily Express* reported, 'Four Bombing Raids on London in nine Hours.' In October, the newspapers reported on 'The Strangest Night—No Air Raids'.

The Brits fought back, chiefly with squadrons of fighters that rose to challenge the bombers. They made the Germans pay a price that had not been paid in their previous invasions in Europe.

'Mass Attacks—Mass Defeats' screamed one headline. The story pointed to scores of enemy planes shot down.

'175 Nazi Planes Down,' said a headline. A sidebar said, 'All day the noise of battle rolled.' The foreign press heavily covered the attacks on London. American journalist Edward R. Murrow reported live via radio for American audiences.

The *New York Sun* reported, 'Britons Calm Under Total War.'

In late July, 1940, the papers reported ominously via British intelligence sources: 'Hitler Seals Off Invasion Bases.' The story said that the German military had shut off all outside access to ports and inland military staging areas in northern France. All outsiders were forbidden entry into the zone. Was this the prelude to the feared invasion?

It would have been if British air defenses had been overcome. But the 'Few', the Royal Air Force pilots, were continuing to hold their own against the *Luftwaffe.*

The British papers reported the analysis of American journalist William Shirer. He pointed to the 'rage' felt by Hitler and Mussolini against Churchill for holding on and fighting on against all odds.

'After all,' Shirer wrote, 'the other nations had surrendered or quit.'

In the meantime the British continued to hit back, with bomber raids deep into Germany. This further infuriated Hitler who had vowed to keep the German people safe.

'Soon We May Bomb Berlin by Day,' said a headline. Night raids were now regular features of RAF tactics. In early October, 1940, the London papers reported on a meeting between Hitler and Mussolini held in the Alps. There, the two dictators vowed, 'Uncompromising defeat of the British Empire, allowing Britain no breathing space.'

Mussolini wanted an invasion of Britain. His troops were meeting defeat against the British in North Africa. Hitler was growing less enthusiastic.

The Photographs

The press made far more use of photos and film than ever before. Some photos became the enduring symbols of London in the war. At the top of the list is the photo of the dome of St. Paul's cathedral during a night raid. The dome is surrounded by the smoke and flames of a burning city, yet it stands unscathed.

A color picture shows a red double-decker bus completely swallowed up by a bomb crater. Many of the famous shots were taken around Fleet Street, the Financial District, and the Strand and in the docklands area. These included the firefighters and air raid and rescue personnel, in their helmets, battling the massive fires that burned whole districts.

Another picture showed citizens, including women and children, sleeping in the subway tunnels and on the platforms to escape the bombing. Some sleep by the disconnected electric third rail. In one photo a little girl clutches her doll while she sits amid the ruins of her house. A Messerschmitt twin-engine bomber, shot down, sits on a London street as a curiosity. A young man reads a book inside a wrecked London bookstore. A department store in Oxford Circus stands ripped open by the bombs.

One picture shows a famous church near Fleet Street completely engulfed in flame from street level to the top of the steeple. This was Christopher Wren's Church of St. Clement Danes, famous for the nursery rhyme, *Oranges and Lemons say the Bells of St. Clement's*. The church was destroyed and not rebuilt for 17 years. The renewed church was dedicated to the Royal Air Force, and contains many air force memorials.

One Plaque, in the ancient language of Latin, describes the modern plight:

DIRUERUNT AERII BELLI FULMINA AD MCMXLI
'Destroyed by the thunderbolts of air warfare—1941'

Outside are the statues of the two men who epitomized air warfare and its 'thunderbolts'. Air Chief Marshal Hugh Dowding commanded Fighter Command, 'the Few', the pilots who fought off the air onslaught and killed the invasion plan.

The other statue honors the man who took the bombing attack to the enemy, and made it even more terrible. Air Marshal 'Bomber' Harris sent thousand-bomber raids over Germany with the purpose of destroying German cities, killing war workers, and breaking the morale needed to continue the fight. His tactic generated great controversy, but Churchill supported it. Harris justified the blanket bombing by saying, "The Germans thought they were going to bomb everyone else. They sewed the wind. They reaped the whirlwind."

Nearby on Fleet Street is a statue of Dr. Samuel Johnson, one of the first 'journalists', who compiled the first real English dictionary, and became a quote machine of the first rank, as reported by his biographer, Boswell. Johnson said only a fool writes for anything other than money. The press barons of Fleet Street would agree. He'd be surprised to learn that modern 'journals' are mostly digital blips on integrated computer circuits.

All around, modern London rises from the wartime ruins. Its population, risen to 8.5 million, is back where it was during World War II. Johnson would doubtlessly approve of what happened to his city after the scourge of war.

"Sir," he said, "when a man is tired of London, he is tired of life."

The Ministry of Truth

It is said that the first casualty of war is truth. It's also true that a nation fighting for its life has little incentive to allow unfettered distribution of any and all bad news about defeats, losses, movements of ships or troops, or plans and policies. In other words, governments want to control or influence news, information, access to sources, and public opinion. They want to get in the business of propaganda, even if it is 'good' propaganda. They want to censor and keep secrets in the name of security.

In 1939, at the declaration of war, the London government created the new Ministry of Information 'to influence national and foreign opinion' about the war, to distribute news and information, and to act as a censor of information that might hurt national security or even morale. It would be the purveyor of 'national propaganda at home and abroad'. In the early days, the MOI was a bit heavy-handed and was criticized for it. The agency was accused of blocking stories, of hectoring and lecturing the public in its campaigns, and of 'snooping' on the public in the guise of monitoring public opinion.

Several ministers came and went, but finally the government settled on Brendan Bracken, a close colleague of Churchill. He curbed the excesses, tried to protect free speech, and assist the press with background information. MOI sponsored films, published posters, magazines, millions of books, assisted with radio shows, and carried out opinion surveys. It air dropped newspapers in occupied Europe, with the help of the RAF, along with tens of millions of propaganda leaflets. A Political Warfare branch produced 'fake' German soldiers' magazines in German and dropped them on German troops. The text promoted the idea of divisions among German generals and leaders.

An army of censors, 12,000 in number, read mail and telegrams to make sure no vital information reached the enemy. This was highly controversial but the supporters, including Bracken, said it kept news of the D-Day Normandy invasion from reaching the Germans.

It tried to influence foreign opinion, particularly in the United States through British Information Service offices at Rockefeller Center in New York, in Chicago, Washington, San Francisco, Los Angeles, and Ottawa, Canada. These offices sent out information to American outlets about the British war effort, the sacrifices and deprivation of the people, the rationing, and the drive to produce more tanks, planes and guns. It aimed to show that Britain was a vital ally of the United States that was doing its part to win the war.

Bracken moved carefully in 'propagandizing' the United States. "We are not a propaganda machine," he said. He added that propaganda would not go well with American media. "It will wind up in the wastepaper basket."

Instead, he wanted the offices to be a resource, a news source to answer questions and inquiries. This turned out to be highly effective, as American reporters, editors and radio journalists sought answers from the offices.

He deplored the fact that Americans and Britons knew little about each other and their institutions, including the American Constitution. The British worried about unfavorable American attitudes toward Britain as an 'Imperial Power' with colonies, possessions, and rule over vast India.

When thousands of American soldiers, sailors and airmen poured into Britain in the buildup to the invasion of Europe, the ministry took on the task of welcoming the Americans and making them feel 'at home'. This mostly involved organizing local groups, social clubs, the Red Cross, and private groups that would provide localized services, receptions, and entertainments.

Bracken, like a lot of Britons, truly welcomed the Americans, despite the occasional complaint that they were 'oversexed, overfed, and over here'.

"The gaiety and kindliness of the Americans will never be forgotten," he said.

The British persuaded Stalin to let the ministry publish a Russian-language weekly newspaper in Moscow, *The British Ally*, which reached a circulation of 50,000 and a readership estimated at 500,000. Bracken was criticized for not ripping into the Germans and Japanese with greater ferocity. He resisted that, on the belief that their often brutal actions spoke for themselves with a grim eloquence mere propaganda could not match. In a Parliamentary debate he had particularly harsh words for the Japanese, "Savages. They are brutal savages."

The MOI was disbanded after the war on the theory that a propaganda agency was not appropriate in peacetime. Arthur Baxter, member of Parliament, said that when the agency gave back the huge university building where it was housed, these words should be carved over the door, '*Here Dwelt the Harlot Propaganda.*' George Orwell, who went on to write the famous dystopian novel, *Nineteen-Eighty-Four*, used the MOI as his model for the novel's Ministry of Truth.

London calling...
George Orwell broadcasts
to India in World War II
DEHLI
BBC
BBC World Service
Bush House
London W.C. 2

Chapter 9
'This Is London calling...'

Broadcasting Ideology to the Wide World

Just up the road from the Fleet Street heart of London journalism stands Bush House, a massive stone edifice in classical style. When it was built in the 1920s by an American businessman, it was billed as the most expensive office building in the world.

Throughout the war Bush House was home to the vast foreign broadcasting service of the BBC—the Overseas Service. The European Service was the most prominent part of the propaganda effort, and turned out 129 programs a day in 24 languages.

Many famous writers and editors worked at Bush House. Some 1,500 journalists, news announcers, on-air presenters, commentators worked there to send news, ideas, commentaries and entertainment across the world in three dozen languages. The aim was to win the war, inform captive peoples, re-assure friends, and provide a touch of home for English-speakers.

In remote jungles, in mountain ranges, on tropical islands, on ships at sea folks could tune their radios to numerous frequencies to hear the comforting sound, *This is London calling…* This was followed by familiar call signals, the live clock chimes of London's Big Ben; a snatch of march music, typically *Lilliburlero*. The world broadcasters wound up at Bush House, where they would remain until 2007, because of the bombing.

Early in the Blitz a giant German bomb, called a mine, landed near BBC headquarters at Broadcasting House in the West End. It caused a 7-hour blaze that forced broadcasters out. It was then the foreign services were sent to Bush House. Soon, the Overseas Service was broadcasting in most European languages, Arabic, several languages of India, Chinese, Spanish—34 in all. Every day the service sent out 250,000 words of news, features, and commentaries.

Bush House was kept secret, it could not even be mentioned by name in Parliament or elsewhere. The fear was the Germans would pinpoint the location and send 500 bombers to wipe it out.

In the war years the most critical division at Bush House was the European Service, which broadcast to all the nations occupied by the Nazis or allied to the Nazis. Among the chief languages were French, German, Dutch, Italian, Polish, Greek, and Danish. Because Russia became an ally, the BBC did not broadcast in Russian. The European Service built a giant transmitter at Spurn Head on the North Sea Coast to cover all of Europe. The station, with 200,000 watts of power, claimed to be the world's most powerful.

This station broadcast the famous Morse code signal, *da-da-da-DAAAH*, the 'V for Victory' along with the opening bars of Beethoven's Fifth Symphony. The European Service's German and French language programs proved to be vital. A number of famous people worked for the German Service, including Hugh Carlton Greene, bother of writer Graham Greene who was in the Intelligence Service. Nobel laureate novelist Thomas Mann worked in the service, as did actor Herbert Lom, who would go on to achieve world-wide fame as the long-suffering boss of Inspector Clouseau in the *Pink Panther film* comedies.

The German Service had a problem early on. A number of the staff were German Jews who had escaped persecution. Should they be put on the air? The decision was made to let them write, produce, report, but not appear before the microphone. The justification was that the BBC should reflect British views and goals and not become a voice for refugees or ethnic victims.

The French service had close ties to the French government in exile, and to the Special Operations Executive, what some called the British government's secret department of dirty tricks. The service, Radio Londres—London, reached a potential audience of millions. Listeners loved its opening—*Ici Londres! Les Francais parlent aux Francais*. 'This is London—the French speaking to the French.'

The Free French leader, General Charles de Gaulle, spoke on the radio to the French people, and famously told his countrymen, "We have lost a battle. We have not lost the war."

Churchill, who spoke French quite well, also addressed the French people by radio. He purposely let his French sound a little rough to seem more authentic. One of the French broadcasters was Maurice Schumann, who would become a future French Foreign Minister.

The SOE, with its network of spies, saboteurs and partisans on the Continent used Radio Londres to send coded messages to agents and resistance fighters. These were read at the end of news broadcasts. Hundreds were sent. A typical message: '*Mademoiselle caresse la nez de son chien.*' 'The lady caresses the nose of her dog.'

'Le lapin a bu un aperitif.' 'The rabbit drank an aperitif.'

On the eve of the Normandy Invasion of Europe, D-Day, the radio offered a passage from a poem by Verlaine: '*Blessent mon coeur d'une langueur monotone.*' 'Wound my heart with a monotonous languor.'

That signaled to thousands of resistance fighters that an invasion was imminent.

Bush House also broadcast a special service to the Netherlands called *Radio Orange*. Queen Wilhelmina, living in exile near London, gave 34 radio speeches to her countrymen on *Radio Orange*. London-based *Radio Belgique* broadcast to occupied Belgium. This service pioneered the use of the V for Victory call signal with the Beethoven accompaniment.

One of the most powerful messages broadcast made by the European Service was an address by Winston Churchill to the Italian people. Italy's dream of a new Roman Empire under Mussolini was fading fast, and Italian disillusionment was growing. Churchill heaped praise on the Italian people, their history, and their culture. But his assessment of Mussolini was scathing, withering and unsparing. He said, "*One man—Mussolini—has led your country to the horrid verge of ruin; one man has arrayed the trustees and inheritors of ancient Rome upon the side of the ferocious pagan barbarians.*"

The Gate of the Year

Radio was powerful and reached across the world. In a way it became a glue binding people together. A whole nation, and vast overseas realms, could all hear the same message at once, and sense the same unity.

At Christmas 1939, on the eve of destruction and all-out war, King George VI gave a traditional holiday speech via radio. Before he spoke, his daughter, Princess Elizabeth, handed him a poem that had gained popularity. He used it in the broadcast. The poem had been written some years before by Minnie Louise Haskins, a lecturer in sociology at the London School of Economics.

The King famously suffered from a speech impediment, a stutter, which he had overcome with therapy. Now the broadcast went out to people who were afraid, and who faced the prospect of grim and protracted war. The King's speech went out to the United Kingdom, to Australia, to remote corners of India, to South Africa, to obscure Pacific islands, and famous Caribbean islands, and all the other dominions, mandates, dependencies, protectorates, and colonies.

At the end of the broadcast, the King spoke slowly and deliberately in the King's English: *"I said to the man who stood at the gate of the year, give me a light that I may tread safely into the unknown. And he replied, 'Go out into the darkness and put your hand into the hand of God. That shall be to you better than light and safer than a known way.'"*

The Power of Listening

The Overseas Service didn't just send out broadcasts, it also listened to broadcasts from the enemies—Germany, Italy, and Japan. A special monitoring section was set up at Caversham, west of London.

The monitors picked up broadcasts from Berlin that were being sent out to radio stations all over Europe on a special frequency. These were news feeds sent at dictation speed. The British grabbed the information, translated it and put it on the air before the German and other European stations could broadcast it.

The Germans were shocked. It seemed the British knew what was happening in Germany before the Germans knew. Goebbels and the Propaganda Ministry scrambled to find where the leaks were coming from. It was a small victory, but a satisfying one.

The BBC 'listeners' at Caversham were the first to pick up the news of the D-Day invasion of Europe by the Allies. They heard the news from German stations and others on the Continent. On D-Day some 725 American radio stations picked up accounts of the invasion from the BBC.

The King's English

A vast volume of international broadcasts from London went out in English. The BBC's philosophy at the time was that the service's English had to be the best in the world, the clearest, with the best pronunciation, and intonation. This went by various names: The King's English, Oxbridge English, and RP—the Received Pronunciation. The announcers and news readers spoke formally, in non-accented English that some called 'the voice of God'. They also seemed unflappable, and could deliver disastrous news with a certain re-assuring calmness and detachment.

The Real Ministry of Truth

Not everything at Bush House went smoothly. One writer grew disillusioned with his job in the broadcast service aimed at India and Burma, the vast British possessions in Asia that would soon be threatened by the Japanese and that already were restless and dreaming of freedom from the British *Raj*.

George Orwell had been born in India and later served in the Imperial Burmese Police. He was educated in England, and went back to Asia. When he came back to England, he worked at various jobs and decided to pursue a writing career. He was drawn to the life of ordinary working people and often wrote about them. In Spain, he fought in the Spanish Civil War.

When World War II broke out, he joined the Home Guard, and later was hired by the BBC India and Eastern Service to produce radio programs broadcast to India to counter Nazi propaganda and anti-Imperial sentiments. He worked at Bush House. In writing programs he elicited support from well-known literary figures, T. S. Eliot, Dylan Thomas, and E. M. Forster.

After two years he began to have doubts about his propaganda efforts. He considered himself a man of the left and aligned with the working class. But he had little use for large bureaucracies and impersonal organizations. He was skeptical of Stalin and the Soviet Union, even though Britain was allied with Russia. He feared totalitarian impulses of the left and right. He could see that India and its 350 million people wanted independence, and a few broadcasts from London were not going to thwart the efforts of Mahatma Gandhi and the Indian Congress Party. Orwell gathered ideas for his future writings, which would change the language, add words and concepts, and chronicle the way propagandists distorted meaning. He saw the future and others would turn his name into an adjective, *Orwellian*.

In the war years he began work on his famous novels, *Animal Farm*, the devastating attack on the Soviet system, and *Nineteen-Eighty-Four*, the vision of a future of endless war, government control, and constantly changing language and meaning. He gave us new words and phrases: *Big Brother, Thought Police, Ministry of Truth, doublespeak,* and the idea that all are equal but some are more equal than others.

The war was no abstraction to Orwell. A German rocket attack so damaged his street he and his wife had to move out of their apartment. Finally, Orwell knew he needed to get out of the propaganda business, even if his propaganda was more defensible than that of the Nazis, Fascists, and Japanese nationalists.

In his resignation letter to the BBC, he said, "I believe in the present political situation the broadcasting of propaganda to India is an almost hopeless task."

Germany Calling

'This is Germany calling. This is Germany calling.'

That's how German Radio (Rundfunk) began its English-language broadcasts to Britain and North America. This was followed by music, then news, which was mostly a litany of British defeats, and later, American defeats or losses. Then there was commentary—propaganda about the failings of Churchill and Roosevelt.

The broadcasts originated from powerful stations in Berlin, Hamburg, Bremen, and other cities that sent signals out in medium wave and short wave bands. Several English speakers made the broadcasts, but one stood out and was on the air from 1940 to 1945. That was William Joyce, known as Lord Haw Haw. His female counterpart was known as Axis Sally.

Lord Haw Haw spoke in upper-class English tones. He sounded rather haughty, and world weary at the same time. He was born in Brooklyn, but was taken to Ireland by his parents, and later went to London. He was educated there and graduated from the University of London.

He joined the British fascists and was strongly pro-German. In 1939, he moved to Germany and became a German citizen. With war coming he was recruited by the German English-language radio service and began broadcasting to Britain. People tuned in to listen, partly out of curiosity, partly from bemusement. His regular audience reached 6 million, as many as 18 million tuned in occasionally.

After Pearl Harbor he claimed that Britain was weak now in all parts of the world and was being replaced by the Americans who would be in effective control of the British Empire, including Canada.

"The British people are too weak to comprehend the catastrophic plight which Churchill has allowed," he said. In his last broadcast from Hamburg, sent out as a great battle swept Berlin and the German Reich collapsed, Lord Haw Haw sounded both inebriated and wistful—what might have been. He lamented that Germany and Britain had never formed an alliance to fight 'Stalin and the menace from the East'.

"My work has been in vain," he said. He signed off: "You may not hear from me again. Long live Germany. Heil Hitler! Farewell."

In a British parody, he yells, "Hell Hitler!" A few days after the last broadcast, Lord Haw-Haw was apprehended near the Danish border by Intelligence agents. He was taken to London, charged with treason, put on trial, and convicted. After failed appeals, he was hanged in London's Wandsworth Prison.

Chapter 10
Capital of Capitals

With a Dozen Exile or Fledgling Governments in London

In the war London was not only the capital of the United Kingdom and the British Empire, it became the *de facto* capital of a dozen nations in exile, or nations that were coming into being, including India, Israel, and Pakistan. The BBC did what it could to accommodate these conquered nations. On Sunday night it broadcast their national anthems.

France

When France fell to the Nazi Blitz warfare in 1940, thousands of French troops escaped to Britain, along with a rising leader, General Charles de Gaulle. He and others established a Free French government in exile in London.

Suddenly, France had four governments: Nazi occupied Northern France, with a capital at Paris; un-occupied southern France under old Marshal Phillipe Pètain, who collaborated with Hitler, with a capital at the spa town of Vichy; The Free French with a capital at London; and the French African colonial possessions with a capital at Algiers.

De Gaulle wanted his country back. He was pitted against Hitler, the Vichy government, and even the fence-sitting French authorities in North Africa. The British provided space for the Free French government in an up-scale building at 4 Carlton Gardens in the elegant St. James district in the heart of the government area.

De Gaulle broadcast a famous 'appeal to the French' on the BBC's French Service: "To all French people: France has lost a battle. France has not lost the war."

He called on the French people to rally around him and 'to act, to sacrifice, and to have hope'.

He adopted a new symbol, the Cross of Lorraine, in honor of Joan of Arc. The cross contrasted with the Nazi 'hooked cross'—the Swastika.

De Gaulle had some success. Some 50 French warships and 170 merchant ships joined the British and Free French cause. By the time of the D-Day invasion the Free French forces numbered some 400,000 troops. They were given the honor of liberating Paris in 1944.

Still, there were rough moments. Churchill and De Gaulle often clashed. There was a real crisis when Churchill ordered British ships in the Mediterranean to attack French battleships anchored in Algeria. He feared they could be used by the Germans to support the invasion of Britain. He could not allow their use, and could not get a commitment to neutralize the ships. The attack destroyed 3 battleships and killed 1000 French sailors.

The Free French fought the Nazis, the Italians, and other Frenchmen, particularly in North Africa, Syria and Lebanon where Vichy French forces resisted the British and Free French. In one case, one regiment of the French Foreign Legion battled another Legion regiment. Ultimately, the Vichy forces were beaten.

Poland

Perhaps no nation in modern times suffered more than Poland. It was attacked by two superpowers, Germany and Soviet Russia. It was occupied, split up, and finally eliminated from the map—literally. The name Poland disappeared, replaced by the name General Government. 3 million Polish Jews died, along with 3 million other Poles, mostly Christians. That was one of every six Poles.

The Polish people did not disappear. They managed to fight on. Thousands of soldiers escaped to fight again. A Home Army, an underground army, kept up the fight. Polish leaders fled to London where they set up a Polish Republic government in exile under General W. Sikorski. The government took over the Polish Embassy on Central London's Portland Place. Later, it spread across buildings around London.

A participant in the exile government was Ignacy Jan Paderewski, former foreign minister and a world-famous concert pianist and composer. He would die in New York while on a fund-raising trip. He was so famous he was given his own star on the Hollywood Walk of Fame.

The Poles brought with them more than just hopes and memories. They brought manpower. Eventually, some 250,000 Polish soldiers, airmen, and sailors would fight with the Allies, usually as part of British commands. After the war, with Poland occupied by the Soviet Union more than 120,000 Polish war veterans chose to stay in Britain permanently.

Even before Poland was invaded several Polish war ships slipped out of the Baltic and escaped to Britain. They fought with the Royal Navy in the Battle of the Atlantic. Polish airmen, flying with the RAF against the German *Luftwaffe*, shot down 526 enemy planes. Some 75,000 Polish troops were formed into the 1st Polish Corps, and included an Armored Division and a Parachute Brigade.

In North Africa and the Middle East, the 2nd Polish Corps was formed, with 60,000 men and women and 264 tanks under the command of General W. Anders. They fought as part of the British Army, and sustained 10,000 casualties, many of them in Italy.

Early on, in 1941, the Polish exile government began reporting on concentration camps, atrocities, and massacres in occupied Poland, including deportations to Auschwitz. In 1942, the exile government published a special report, 'Mass Extermination of Jews in German-Occupied Poland.' The report was sent to all the allied nations.

In 1944, with help from the Polish Home Army and Jewish sources in Poland, the BBC ran numerous accounts of concentration camps, exterminations, SS involvement. BBC even broadcast a list of 'Auschwitz butchers'.

The Archbishop of York, a leader of the Church of England, referred to Polish Jews when he said, "In Poland there is taking place one of the most appalling outrages that the whole history of the world has seen." He added that it amounted to 'a bloody massacre'. Foreign Secretary Anthony Eden warned that 'these crimes will not be forgotten.'

Poles provided vital intelligence information to the British and the Allies throughout the war.

Netherlands

When Holland was overrun, Dutch Queen Wilhelmina escaped to England. She was a friend of King George VI and the Queen. They housed her in an estate near London. A Dutch government in exile set up shop in a large office building, Stratton House, in Piccadilly.

Queen Wilhelmina kept in touch with the Dutch people. She made 34 radio broadcasts via the BBC's *Radio Orange*. The Queen sent her daughter, Juliana and her children to Canada for safety. The fact she would not live under Nazi rule made her popular with the people, some of whom collaborated with the Nazi overlords.

"The Queen seems to be the only man in the Dutch government," quipped Churchill.

The exile government still claimed nominal control over Dutch possessions, including huge Dutch East Indies (Indonesia), and the Caribbean islands of Aruba, Curacao, and South America's Dutch Guiana.

The Dutch in the far-east fought with Britain, the Americans and other allies under a joint command in the fight against the Japanese Empire.

The Japanese invaded the Dutch East Indies and many Dutch people were sent to prison camps for the duration of the war.

Belgium

The Belgian King Leopold III allowed himself to be captured when the Germans invaded. He was put under house arrest for the rest of the war. That seeming surrender angered the Belgian people. The king had to step down after Belgium was liberated.

Prime Minister Hubert Pierlot and part of the cabinet fled to London where they established a government in exile, headquartered at Eaton Square in the plush Belgravia neighborhood of the West End.

Some 15,000 Belgian refugees fled, along with some soldiers. The London exiles claimed control over the Belgian Congo, nearly a million square miles, and the special army there, the *Force Publique*, 40,000 strong.

Norway

This exile story is harrowing, and it cost the British dearly as they tried to rescue the Norwegian king and his government.

The Germans invaded Norway. The British sent a cruiser to take King Haakon and his son Prince Olav to the safety of northern Norway. That period of safety was short-lived, and it was decided to take the king and his government to London.

A task force was sent, led by the heavy cruiser *H.M.S. Devonshire*, to pick up the king. Unfortunately, the task force ran into two heavy German warships. They sank the aircraft carrier, *Glorious*, and two escort ships, with the loss of 1,500 sailors. The king at first stayed in London with the British royal family at Buckingham Palace. Later, Haakon and his exile government settled into offices at 10 Palace Green in Kensington, London.

Haakon kept up morale back home by broadcasting messages via BBC. He also worshiped regularly at the St. Olav Norwegian Church in East London.

Czechoslovakia

After the destruction and dismemberment of his country, President Edvard Benes came to London with a government in exile. Later he moved to Wingrave Manor, 36 miles north of London. His government was housed in offices scattered around London.

Yugoslavia

The Germans invaded Yugoslavia. In June, 194l, young King Peter II of Yugoslavia arrived as a refugee in Jerusalem in the British mandate of Palestine. Later he transferred to London He studied at Cambridge and served in the RAF.

For most of the war he lived at the five-star Claridge Hotel. On July 19, 1945, the British government ceded Suite 212 of the hotel to the Kingdom of Yugoslavia for one day so that the king's child, crown prince Alexander, could be born on Yugoslav territory.

Albania

In 1941, deposed King Zog of Albania arrived in London. He lived at the Hotel Ritz, and then at several country estates. In

1946, after the liberation of the country, the new Communist government abolished the monarchy.

Luxembourg

This small Duchy was overrun by the Germans. Her Royal Highness Grand Duchess Charlotte came with her government to London, to the elegant terrace housing of 27 Wilton Crescent, Belgravia, near the Belgian government in exile.

The Grand Duchess broadcast to her people via the BBC. Her government also entered into to the new Benelux economic union with Belgium and the Netherlands.

Greece

The British rescued Greek King George II from the island of Crete. The king and his exiled government spent the war in British-controlled Cairo, Egypt.

Ethiopia

In the 1930s, Italy's Mussolini was determined to build a new Roman Empire. His forces invaded Ethiopia, a poor but proud nation in the Horn of Africa. Emperor Haile Selassie rallied his nation of 12 million people but they were no match for the modern Italian forces.

In May, 1936 the British cruiser HMS *Enterprise* picked up the emperor and took him to Jerusalem in the British mandate territory of Palestine. From there he was taken to England where he lived in exile until 1941 when British, Commonwealth, and Allied forces swept the Italians out of Ethiopia. At that point the Emperor returned in triumph to his capital at Addis Ababa.

The departure of one emperor still left London and vicinity as the home to six kings and queens, one grand duchess, and several presidents, prime ministers, and provisional heads of state.

The India Problem

Even as London fought to save itself, it could not escape its far-flung responsibilities across the world. At the top of the list was India.

The great and restless subcontinent was home to 400 million people in 700,000 villages and dozens of teeming cities. In the caste system, 50 million 'untouchables' lived in absolute poverty and social isolation. Half the population was malnourished. Every year, the population increased by six million (In the war years the population grew from 350 million to almost 400 million.) For years, the Congress party, Indian nationalists, Hindu and Moslem leaders, agitated for independence. Now in the midst of a world war a whole series of crises impinged on India:

- Famine broke out in Bengal, with an estimated 700,000 deaths.
- The British Army and the British Indian Army were engaged in fierce fighting against the Japanese forces in Northeast India and Burma.
- Indian independence leaders Mahatma Gandhi, Pandit Nehru, and Moslem leader Ali Jinnah continued to push for British assurances that they would 'quit India' when the war was won. Jinnah pushed for partitioning the country, with separation of religious groups into Moslem Pakistan and Hindu Hindustan. Jinnah and his Moslem League took a hard line: end the 'slavery' of British rule, and avoid future domination by the 'Hindu caste system'.
- Communal fighting between Hindus and Moslems could break out at any time.

With exceptions, Indians remained loyal during the war. In fact the British Indian Army, a separate force from the British Army, enrolled two million soldier, the largest volunteer force in the world.

A new viceroy had been appointed, Field Marshal Archibald Wavell, the 'soldier viceroy'. He knew India and had commanded forces defending it. He ordered the army to help in famine relief, with emergency food shipments from Australia, and the inoculation and vaccination of millions against cholera and smallpox.

In London, the government was divided over India. Churchill was a champion of Empire, and did not want to preside over its breakup. He thought British rule was all that kept India from breaking up in sectarian civil war. The opposite sentiment was voiced by Sir George Schuster, a Member of Parliament and former official in the Government of India.

"I want to see India take her place as one of the great nations of the world," he said. Clement Atlee, who would become prime minister after the war, wanted to get Britain out of the empire business.

Despite the war, despite the Japanese attack on India, despite the independence movement, London formulated development plans for India, plans that would take 15 years to complete.

Professor A. V. Hill of Cambridge completed a lengthy survey of India's needs. He concluded that the food supply needed to grow by one-third. He noted the poor health statistics and the low literacy rate for women—8 %.

The long-range development plan, which would begin after the war, contemplated spending billions of dollars over 15 years to transform the villages and drastically boost the food supply. That plan would never see the light of day. In four years, India would be independent. It would happen amid great sectarian strife, and with the creation of two nations: the Republic of India and Pakistan.

Chapter 11
From London to Jerusalem

The Birth of Israel

London was full of governments in exile, representing nations and peoples who were occupied, oppressed and fearful of the future. One nation was waiting to be born. The people and the forces that would create Israel after the war were either concentrated in London or were directed from London.

This was one of history's ironies. Two thousand years ago, the Roman Empire, fed up with the rebellious vassal province of Israel, kicked the Jews out of their own country. At that same time the Romans were conquering the island of Britain—Britannia; and founding the city of Londinium—London. Now a new empire was in a position to redress the wrongs of that long-dead empire.

One man who had championed a new Jewish state was buried in an obscure grave in a London cemetery. He had befriended and supported Hungarian-born Theodor Herzl, who had founded the Zionist movement and proposed a Jewish homeland in 1896 in a book, *The Jewish State*.

Herzl's chief supporter, William Hechler, was a scholar and a fighter against anti-Semitism. He was also a Christian pastor in the Church of England. Hechler moved between London and Vienna where he was chaplain for the British Embassy. He had contacts in the German-speaking world and in London. He helped Herzl promote the idea of a Jewish homeland. Those efforts were futile. Herzl died of heart disease at the young age of 44. He told Hechler, "Greet Palestine for me. I gave my heart's blood for my people."

As the years wore on after Herzl's death, more people took up the cause of a Jewish state.

The man who would become the first president of the State of Israel was living and working in London. The man who would be credited as the founder of Israel, and its first prime minister, was commuting on the London subway.

The man who first proposed a British-led establishment of a Jewish homeland and nation of Israel was himself a member of the British ruling establishment—and a Jew. The latter gentleman sported the rather impressive title, Sir Herbert Samuel, the Viscount Samuel, GCB, OM, GBE, PC.

The first president of Israel, Chaim Weizmann, also a British citizen, was also a member of the British establishment—one of the nation's top military researchers and friend of Churchill, Clement Atlee, and other high members of the government.

Weizmann also headed the World Zionist Organization, with the goal of finding a homeland for the world's Jews. He had influential supporters, scientists, politicians, and the powerful editor C. P. Scott of the *Manchester Guardian.*

Another Zionist and strong supporter of a new Israel was Harold Laski, a secular Jew and a leading British political theorist, author, lecturer and a hero of the Left who influenced a generation of politicians through his books and professorship at the London School of Economics.

The Archbishop of Canterbury, leader of the Church of England, co-founded the Council of Christians and Jews to fight anti-Semitism. In 1943, he told the House of Lords, "Jews are being slaughtered at the rate of tens of thousands a day on many days." He called for immediate action to help Jews. At that point in the war the British were locked in battles with Hitler in the Atlantic and in North Africa, but they did control Palestine, the future Jewish homeland.

The man who would be credited as the 'founder of Israel', David Ben-Gurion, was a former British soldier. He was living in London. He saw the Blitz bombing and greatly admired the stoicism and tenacity of the Londoners under fire. The British struggled to survive the onslaught and maintain their independence at all cost. Ben-Gurion would lead a new nation faced with similar requirements.

He certainly was not a part of the British establishment. In fact, he would be a bit of a thorn in the British side before, during, and after the war.

Ben-Gurion's great goal was to get Jewish refugees from Nazi-controlled Europe and elsewhere into Palestine. That growing Jewish population would form the basis for a new state of Israel.

The British, who controlled Palestine, struggled to keep some kind of peaceful balance between the growing Jewish population and the Arab residents. It was a thankless task that seemed to inflame both sides. As Britain itself tried to survive bombing, blockades, and invasion threats, the British in Palestine had to deal with the explosive tensions between Jewish settlers and the Palestinian Arabs.

In Parliament, a member asked the government spokesman to 'clarify' British rules dealing with prayer at the Wailing Wall in Jerusalem, the rights and responsibilities of Jews and Moslems, and whether Jews could blow the Ram's Horn at the Wall. It's the kind of question that is still being asked today.

Members of Parliament also raised questions about the actions of the British Palestine Police, which was now a part of the military. Were they anti-Jewish, anti-Arab? One official with wide experience there explained, "The place is an appalling mess. It's a delicate balancing act." He explained, "The Palestine Administration had to deal with three Sabbaths, Jewish, Moslem, and Christian, a festival every other day, and three languages, Hebrew, Arabic, and English."

Another official claimed, "Under British protection, the tender plant of Zionist colonization has been allowed to germinate, sprout, and flourish." Statements like that further inflamed Arab sensibilities.

Critics in Parliament wondered whether the British might not be screwing things up through a certain clueless and bull-headed stubbornness and arrogance. It had happened before, they noted, in places like the American colonies.

The British were never able to resolve the conflict in the Middle East, and the fighting between the two sides continues to this day.

A Stunning Proposal

In many ways the roots of this struggle go back to World War I and a proposal made by Herbert Samuel, a Jew from

Liverpool, a key politician in the British parliament, a future Home Secretary in the cabinet, and a leader of the Liberal Party.

He also wanted a National State for Jews. The old Ottoman Empire, run from Turkey, was on the verge of falling apart. The British and their allies were helping it collapse through military action, sabotage, the incitement to rebellion.

The Arabs were in revolt, helped by famed Arab expert, Lawrence of Arabia. Palestine, controlled by the Ottomans, was ripe for picking. Samuel, who was an unabashed Imperialist, circulated a remarkable plan in the British cabinet. He proposed that when the Ottoman Empire fell apart, the British should annex Palestine into the British Empire and then create an autonomous Jewish state. He said it was the British obligation to 'civilize' these lesser lands and bring British values to the former Ottoman provinces.

Samuel envisioned a Jewish state with 3 or 4 million Jews in its ancient homeland where they would 'draw on the 1,500 years of greatness before the diaspora'. He said, "This Jewish homeland may again enrich the world."

Under British protection, this semi-autonomous state would be open to the world, and to development, and would guarantee the safety of Jews, Christians, Moslems, and the peace and accessibility of the Holy Places.

His plan didn't get very far. War was raging in Europe, and the Ottomans were not beaten. But two years later, the British government issued the famous Balfour Declaration, named after the foreign secretary, which called for the establishment of a Jewish homeland in Palestine. It didn't say how or when. However, at this point the British were in control of Palestine, the Ottomans were out, and Jews and Arabs both had renewed hopes and ambitions.

In 1920, Samuel was named British High Commissioner of Palestine, the first Jew to rule there in some 2,000 years. The Arab population was not pleased, and claimed the appointment represented 'an alliance between British colonialism and Zionism'.

In the 1920s and '30s, the juggling and struggling increased. More Jews settled in Palestine. David Ben-Gurion headed the Jewish Agency charged with bringing them in and getting them settled. The rise of Hitler made this work all the more vital. Over the years, the agency would create whole new towns and communities in what would become Israel.

There was one huge stumbling block: the Arabs believed the Jewish influx was being imposed on them by an Imperial Britain and a guilt-ridden west determined to help oppressed Jews at all costs—costs to them.

The British tried to satisfy both sides and satisfied no one. They were forced to keep an army in the area, the Ninth Army, in part to keep the two sides apart. They curtailed Jewish immigration, which led to smuggling and defiance.

Then disaster hit Europe as World War II broke out and Hitler's armies swept across Europe. Suddenly, these armies were poised on the English Channel and threatening to invade Britain. Even as Britain faced this existential threat British forces continued the fight in North Africa, the Middle East, and the Horn of Africa. The question of a Jewish homeland now seemed of marginal importance to London.

In 1940, '41, and '42, British and Commonwealth forces fought across North Africa, from Morocco to Egypt; in the Horn of Africa against Mussolini's Fascist forces, and in the Middle East; in Syria, and Lebanon where Free French and Vichy French forces clashed. They fought in Greece and the eastern Mediterranean.

The British kept forces in Palestine, not just to keep Arabs and Jewish settlers apart, but also to protect Jews if Nazi forces pushed all the way across Egypt and the Suez Canal.

In an echo of today's news, the British dispatched an army, the Tenth Army, to Iraq to depose a rogue government backed by Hitler. Fighting took place in Basra, Mosul, Falluja, Ramadi—names that would be familiar battlegrounds 65 years later.

Jews in Palestine and the Middle East wanted to fight Hitler. By 1940 there were nearly 500,000 Jews in Palestine, up from 80,000 or so 20 years earlier. Jews were around 30% of the population. The British formed Jewish military units within the British 8th Army in North Africa. They rejected creating separate Jewish forces. Later in the war they did create a Jewish Brigade of 5,000 soldiers under British Jewish commanders. The brigade fought in Europe. In Britain itself, there was a special

Commando Special Forces unit consisting of Jewish refugees. In all, about 40,000 Jews served in the British forces during the war.

These Jewish troops would form the backbone of the Israeli Armed Forces, the IDF, and would include 35 future generals. Some of these ex-soldiers would take up arms against the British administration in Palestine to force the birth of Israel.

One soldier trained by the British would go on to become an Israeli war hero, head of the IDF, and defense minister. Moshe Dayan was mentored by British officer Orde Wingate, who would enjoy great fame fighting the Japanese in India and Burma with his Special Forces jungle fighters. Wingate was stationed in Palestine, and organized special Jewish militias to counter Arab insurgents. One of his recruits was Moshe Dayan.

Wingate was an outspoken Zionist, which got him in trouble with his superior officers back in London. In London, Chaim (Charles) Weizmann was proving he was a true patriot of his adopted country. His scientific work as head of the Royal Navy laboratories was producing results that would help win the war. That included improved explosives, high octane gasoline, chemical fermentation, and production of synthetic products.

While wearing his Zionist Organization hat, he lobbied the top levels of the British government for action on a Jewish state and on refugees. He was such a prominent Briton that his name was in the Black Book of the SS; the register of those Britons to be arrested and eliminated.

Then, Weizmann paid a heavy price. His son, Flight Lt. Michael Weizmann, a pilot in the RAF, was shot down and killed in 1942 fighting Nazi-ism. His body was never found, a reality his father could never accept. Weizmann soldiered on. Working with him in London at the Zionist organization was a young London-educated man who had studied languages, including Arabic at Cambridge. Abba Eban would go on to serve as an officer in British military intelligence in Jerusalem and in Egypt. In the State of Israel, he would serve in the cabinet, then as deputy prime minister. Later, he would serve eight years as Israel's foreign secretary and spokesman on countless issues. His face and 'King's English' would become familiar around the world.

Throughout the war, the Jewish Agency under Ben-Gurion continued to bring refugees to Palestine from Europe. Many were saved from death. They came despite British attempts to curtail the movement of people into the volatile province.

One of those working with Ben-Gurion was an American-born woman who moved to Palestine and worked on a Kibbutz after her formative years in Milwaukee and Denver. Golda Meir would go on to become prime minister of Israel, and will be the first politician to be called 'The Iron Lady'.

Not every Jew who escaped to Palestine found a welcome, or came with a peaceful purpose. Menachem Begin, a Pole who attended the University of Warsaw, got away after the German invasion. He joined the Free Polish forces of General Anders. They would become the II Polish Corps of the British 8th Army. Begin dropped out and stayed in Palestine, as did some other Jewish fighters. They developed the idea that to bring in more refugees, fight off Arab resistance, and force the British to act on the creation of Israel, they had to arm themselves and go underground with military actions.

When the war ended with an Allied victory, the pressure to open Palestine to Holocaust survivors and act on a State of Israel became intense. Begin and other underground fighters launched attacks on the British, who kept thousands of troops in Palestine.

Ben-Gurion was in London when the war ended. He saw the happy celebrations in the streets, the crowds outside Buckingham Palace. He also knew it was time to take a harder line in pushing the British to act on Israel. With millions of his fellow Jews dead, and thousands without a home, the time for niceness and gradualism was over. Ben-Gurion supported defiance, but not violence.

But now there were hardliners—hot heads—who were willing to pick up guns and bombs to further the cause.

In the summer of 1946, Begin's underground group, *Irgun,* planted a huge bomb at the King David Hotel in Jerusalem, headquarters of the British Palestine government and military. Some 91 people died in the blast, including; British citizens, Arabs, and 17 Jews. The terror attack shocked London and the British people, who were weary of war and fighting. The attack was denounced by the press, Parliament, the prime minister, and by Jewish groups, Ben-Gurion, Weizmann, and others. Begin and the Irgun were vilified as 'terrorists and fascists'.

The British cut off all contact with Jewish civilians, and mounted a massive security sweep. Some 20,000 troops and police sealed off Tel Aviv and made hundreds of arrests.

Begin, who used disguises and fake names, was pursued by the police, MI-5, and other authorities. He was banned from Britain, even after Israel became a state.

The attack did not block British and American support for a Jewish state. Churchill, Prime Minister Atlee, and American President Truman still argued for a Jewish state. To this day there is great controversy over whether the Jewish underground warned the British and they ignored the warning, or whether the warning was ever really given to the British officials in the hotel.

In 1947, the British had 100,000 troops in Palestine for a territory with 1.5 million people. In addition, both the Arab and Jewish communities operated armed militias and special police. The two sides clashed despite the British peacekeeping presence.

The Minister for Colonies told the House of Commons that Britain was planning to march away, and withdraw from Palestine. The United Nations would take over, but with little chance of reconciling the two sides.

He explained the British move as, "Faced with Jewish demands and Arab refusal, we could not under the mandate establish either a Jewish state or an Arab state in Palestine by force, nor could we coerce either people in the interest of the other."

He concluded: "It is our prayer that the people in the Holy Land cooperate."

The record showed that since 1920 there had been periodic clashes, attacks, and killings between Jews and Arabs. During all that time the British had control of the territory. And no permanent peace ensued.

In May 1948, the British pulled out of Palestine and ended their mandate rule and deferred to the United Nations. Almost immediately, Jewish leaders, led by David Ben-Gurion, declared the creation and independence of Israel (Eretz Israel).

That was followed by an outbreak of fighting between Jews and Arabs, the flight of many Arabs, and an attack on Israel from the adjoining Arab nations. The conflict and fighting continued into the next century and goes on today.

Begin would go on to become prime minister of Israel, and would enter into a peace accord with Egyptian president Anwar Sadat. Begin and Sadat would be awarded the Nobel Peace prize.

In 1937, the British had proposed creating two states, Israel for Jews and Palestine for the Arabs. No action was taken. That proposal, the two-state solution, is still on the table today.

Chapter 12
Secrets and Spies

The Espionage Capital

Wartime London was full of secrets, secret agencies, secret projects. It was also full of spies searching for secrets, secret agencies, and secret projects.

Spies could remain anonymous in a city teeming with refugees, exiles, deposed officials, and revolutionaries plotting to thwart British rule. There were spies, double-agents, moles, ex-spies, code makers, and code-breakers, counter-spies, disinformation experts, intelligence, and counter- intelligence operatives of all kinds.

There was even a secret government agency responsible for spying, sabotage, assassination, dirty tricks, insurgency, and terrorism using bombs, poison, or any means necessary.

The British intelligence and counter-spy agencies kept a low profile. MI-5, the counter-spies, kept a London headquarters at an office building on St. James Street, with the only sign reading, TO LET. The agency also had major offices at vast Blenheim Palace, Churchill's birthplace near Oxford. The Secret intelligence Service, MI-6, occupied an unmarked building at 54 Broadway, London.

There were not many enemy spies in London. The Germans, Italians, and Japanese had trouble penetrating Britain with their agents. The German spy agency, *Abwehr*, was in disarray, and its leadership ambivalent at best about Hitler and his goals and methods.

Fascist sympathizers in Britain were greatly discredited and suspect after Germany invaded its neighbors and threatened invasion of Britain. The 'appeasers' who tried conciliation had obviously failed and now kept their heads down. They were not trusted.

The successful spies—incredibly successful—were 'friendlies' from allied countries. (More on that later.)

Almost all the German spies in Britain were working for the British agency MI-5. They had been discovered and 'turned' into double agents by the wonderfully named XX Committee—the double cross.

The fact the British had broken the German Enigma code meant that spies were picked up or tracked by MI-5 or the Special Branch of Scotland Yard. Those who weren't turned were caught, tried, and hanged or shot. One made history.

Last in the Tower

German agent Josef Jakobs parachuted into England from a German plane in January, 1941. He landed in a field and broke his ankle. He sought help from some farmers who were suspicious and turned him in to the Home Guard.

He carried L 500, forged I.D. papers, radio transmitter, and a sausage. He was sent to London, put on trial before a military tribunal, and convicted.

He was sent to the Tower of London where he was executed by firing squad from the Scots Guards. He had to sit in a chair because of his broken ankle. He was the last person executed at the Tower of London.

Super- Fast Eddie

Englishman Eddie Chapman had a spy career that would have eclipsed James Bond. He was flamboyant and lived on the edge. He was also a crime figure, safecracker, and underworld associate. With crime money he lived the London high life with celebrity friends.

In 1940, he was hiding out from the police in the Channel Islands when the Germans invaded. Chapman agreed to spy for the *Abwehr* and was parachuted back into England.

Instead of spying he surrendered. He was taken to London to an MI-5 center where he was easily turned into a double agent by master counterspy Lt. Col. 'Tin Eye' Stephens who always wore a monocle.

Chapman had to show the Germans he was doing his job. They wanted him to blow up an aircraft factory. MI-5 decided to fake it. They would 'blow up' the De Haviland bomber factory using special effects, fake ruins, debris, a phony crater, and a planted newspaper story about an explosion.

The Germans bought it. Chapman was a hero. He made it back to Germany where he was awarded an Iron Cross medal, the only British citizen ever to get one.

He survived the war, made it home, wrote three books, and was honored by his home country. More troubling was the story of Tyler Kent, a Princeton-educated cypher clerk at the American embassy in London. He took classified documents out of the embassy, including copies of messages between Churchill and Roosevelt. He was being watched by MI-5 and the Scotland Yard. He had ties to American isolationists and Russian emigres.

Some of the messages wound up in the hands of German intelligence. Kent was caught, tried, and sentenced to seven years in prison.

Some of the spy stories were more sad than menacing. Duncan Scott-Ford was a 21-year-old seaman in the Merchant Navy. He sold information to German agents when his ship was in port in Portugal. Then he did it again. The usefulness of the data was questionable, but officials were afraid agents would recruit seamen.

He eventually was arrested, tried, found guilty, and hanged as a traitor. He was paid about $1,600 in current money.

Last Days of Hitler

In April of 1945, 2.5 million Russian soldiers surrounded Berlin and were fighting toward the center of the city, the site of the Reich government and Hitler's bombproof bunker.

The Russians captured the city. What happened to Hitler? Was he dead, did he escape? Rumors were flying and the Russians did little to dispel the rumors. British intelligence, MI-6 assigned one of their agents in Berlin, historian Hugh Trevor-Roper, to find out what happened to Hitler.

Trevor-Roper tracked down many of the Nazis, military officers, officials, and staff, including secretaries, who were in the bunker in the last days. He interviewed as many as he could and gathered interview information from other intelligence officers.

The result was the definitive work on what happened to Hitler, his marriage to Eva Braun, his thoughts on impending defeat, his farewell to his followers, and finally the suicide of Hitler and his now wife by pistol and cyanide, followed by the burning of the bodies. Trevor-Roper included details, such as the poisoning of the Fuhrer's dog, Blondi, the reaction to the death of Mussolini and the rage against the Nazi leaders still on the loose and grabbing power.

Trevor-Roper published this as, *The Last Days of Hitler*, which became a best-seller and the basis for books, movies, TV shows, and documentaries that are still being made.

The Last Prisoner in the Tower

There was one strange incident in the war that no intelligence officer, journalist or historian has been able to figure out for sure.

In May 1941, the man who had risen with Hitler almost from the beginning, who was at his side at the great party rallies, and who was thought to be the most faithful of all made a move that shocked both sides.

Rudolph Hess, deputy Fuhrer, a man at the top of state and party power, got into a Messerschmitt fighter plane, which he piloted, and flew alone to Britain, specifically to the estate in Scotland of the Duke of Hamilton, an aristocratic flying enthusiast who knew Nazi leaders and Churchill.

The Duke was also air commodore and wing commander Lord Hamilton of the RAF, and chief of air defense for Scotland and Northern England. He had three brothers in the air force.

In 1936, at the Berlin Olympics, Lord Hamilton had met Göring, Hitler, Von Ribbentrop, and others. He was a Member of Parliament and knew British politics. Hess planned to broker a peace deal between Germany and Britain. He seemed to discount the fact that thousands of German planes had been attacking British cities and hundreds of submarines were sinking hundreds of British ships. Hess had a hard time finding the landing strip at Dungavel Castle, and tried to land in the wrong place. With his parachute on he bailed out as the plane crashed in the night. He was slightly injured. Local farmers turned him over to the Home Guard who passed him on to the military. Hess met with Hamilton and the Duke called Churchill.

Churchill showed no interest in negotiating with Hess. Hess was handled as a prisoner of war. For a time he was locked up in the Tower of London, the state prison that had held English queens, rebels, and aristocrats such as Sir Walter Raleigh. Hess was the last prisoner to be held in the Tower.

The Germans immediately denounced Hess and claimed he 'went crazy' and acted alone. Hess spent the rest of the war at a military hospital and P.O.W center in the hills of Wales. He was tried at Nuremberg after the war and sentenced to life in prison. He died in 1987 in Berlin.

To this day, the reasons for the flight remain a mystery as the *Telegraph* newspaper says it is 'shrouded in mystery and speculation'.

One theory says British Intelligence was involved, and that's why the air space was unguarded. Documents found in Russia indicate Hitler knew about the plan, and that Hess wanted Britain to join Germany to fight Stalin and the Soviet Union. If so, then Hess could imagine the unimaginable—an alliance between Churchill and Hitler.

The Dublin Dilemma

The Republic of Ireland declared neutrality in the war, a move that got London's attention in a big way. Would Ireland become a hotbed of German espionage and intrigue? Would German submarines drop agents on Irish shores? Would the violent Irish Republican Army accept support from Hitler?

Ireland was not so much pro-German as it was wary of Britain, which had ruled Ireland for centuries. The reality was that the Irish government did not want to be seen as hostile to Britain. The Irish arrested spies and saboteurs. It quietly cooperated with the British in many ways, without strictly renouncing neutrality.

The German embassy remained open throughout the war, and the German ambassador, Eduard Hempel, sent thousands of messages and reports to Berlin. It was not some vast center of spying and intelligence as some in the British government feared.

At the end of the war in Europe, with Hitler defeated, members of Parliament demanded that the Irish government arrest the 'nest of spies' in the German embassy in Dublin. A Foreign Office spokesman pointed out that the German embassy currently had a staff of 11 people, half of them clerks and secretaries. They were not arrested.

The Great Spy Ring

Hostile spies had a hard time, but there were plenty of 'friendly' spies. Britain was now allied with Stalin and the Soviet Union in the fight against Hitler. There were plenty of pro-Soviet sympathizers and allies among the political left in Britain. They did more than sympathize. They were willing to help, to pass along secrets, to propagandize for the 'brave Soviet ally' facing the full force of Hitler's armies and Blitz warfare. The supporters were often disillusioned with capitalism and the West, and were starry-eyed about the Communist vision of a 'working class Utopia' of fairness and equality.

Churchill, certainly no fan of Marxism, said that if Hitler invaded Hell he'd put in a good word for the devil.

For many on the British left Soviet Russia seemed to be the wave of the future. They had the capacity to simply overlook the planned famines, the purges, and the exiles sent to Siberia.

This attitude and opportunity gave rise to one of the most successful—and damaging—spy rings in history. These spies were well-educated Britons, often from the upper class, with high level jobs in government or science; with easy access to intelligence sources, and to allies, particularly the Americans. They penetrated the Foreign Office, the Secret Intelligence Service, the Security Service (MI-5), the Army, the BBC, the code-breaking program, and top secret science projects, including the atom bomb.

These spies passed on secrets that would threaten world-wide destruction. One spy may have done as much damage as any spy in history. Klaus Fuchs, a man of the German left and fiercely anti-Nazi, escaped to Britain after Hitler came to power.

He was a brilliant theoretical physicist and mathematician working on atomic theory. He soon was working with top British scientists at Bristol, Edinburgh, and Birmingham. These included Max Born, a German refugee, and Rudolf Peierls.

Fuchs was recruited to work on the top-secret *Tube Alloys*, the code name for an atomic bomb. He began passing secrets to the Soviet Union via 'Sonia'—Ruth Kuczinski, a major in Soviet military intelligence. He traveled to London to meet his contact.

He became a British citizen. British atomic researchers worked with the Americans on the Manhattan atomic bomb project. Fuchs went to Los Alamos, New Mexico, the secret ‘atomic city’ where he became a leading member of the team building the first atom bomb. He worked with Hans Bethe, the top theoretician. Fuchs developed new science on implosion—the triggering of a chain reaction explosion. It was critical research.

He was an associate of other famous scientists, John Von Neumann, Richard Feynman. Fuchs was there at Trinity site when the first atom bomb was tested.

He went on spying. He passed more secrets to the Soviets. His spy contact was Harry Gold, who played a role in a second famous spy case—Julius and Ethel Rosenberg, American spies executed for passing atomic secrets from Los Alamos to the Soviets.

After the war, Fuchs returned to Britain where he became head of theoretical physics at the new Harwell Atomic Research Establishment. Now he was working on an even more deadly bomb: the hydrogen bomb. He continued to pass secrets. He was almost caught and eventually was caught. Still, it was a source of endless embarrassment to the British to know much of their nuclear program was being run by a spy.

He was tried for treason, convicted, and served part of his sentence. He then moved to Communist East Germany where he was treated as a hero and heaped with awards. He went on to advise the Communist Chinese on how to build an atomic bomb. Hans Bethe, the atomic theorist at Los Alamos, said that Fuchs ‘changed history’.

Another British atom spy, Alan Nunn May, a physicist, would be one of the small army of Soviet spies who worked or studied at Cambridge University.

May was associated with the great Cavendish Lab at Cambridge where so many atomic and physics breakthroughs were accomplished by giants, such as J. J. Thomson, Ernest Rutherford, Lord Rayleigh, and others.

May was recruited by James Chadwick, Nobel laureate, to work on *Tube Alloys*, the atom bomb project. He worked on Chadwick’s atomic reactor project.

He passed secrets on to the Soviet Union, including samples of vital uranium isotopes. He was arrested in London as a spy, convicted, and sentenced.

Fuchs, May and a host of other British spies working for the Soviets did a lot to damage U.S.-British relations and cooperation. American officials grew wary of telling the British too much for fear the information would wind up in Moscow. They were right.

Cambridge Clique

A whole clique of spies with ties to Cambridge University represented a spectacular success for Soviet military and civilian intelligence agencies.

These men wormed their way into the heart of the British civil service, the diplomatic corps, the military and intelligence establishment. They passed on military secrets, plans and policies, information on code-breaking, scientific and technical secrets.

The best known of these were:

Kim Philby
Guy Burgess
Donald Maclean
Anthony Blunt.

They have been the subject of books, movies, articles, TV programs, documentaries, both factual, and fictionalized. More than one spy story has relied on the histories of these superspies.

Perhaps the most remarkable of the superspies was Kim Philby, born in India, educated in England at Cambridge. He managed to work as a mole, a double-agent, and won awards from both sides.

He was recruited early—in the 1930s—as a Soviet spy. He worked as a Fleet Street journalist and traveled around Europe, served as a war correspondent in Spain during the Civil War, and was even given a medal by General Franco.

During the war he got a job with the Special Operations Executive, the secret agency set up to create chaos and to infiltrate Nazi-held territories.

He moved over to the Secret Intelligence Service, the spy agency, where he controlled a network of agents throughout southern Europe. He passed vital information to Moscow about

German invasion plans and British code-breaking successes at Bletchley Park.

He was given the Order of the British Empire in 1946. Later, he moved to Washington where he was chief of intelligence at the British Embassy and worked closely with the CIA, and had dealing with James Jesus Angleton, CIA's chief of counter-intelligence.

Angleton, who went to school in England and served a tour of duty in London, had suspicions about Philby early on. Philby came close to being caught several times. There were missed signs and strange co-incidences that would have incriminated Philby.

Slowly the ring began to close around Philby as other Cambridge spies, Guy Burgess and Donald Maclean, were about to be caught. Philby beat the rap by fleeing to Moscow. He was given Soviet citizenship, a pension and an apartment. A stamp honoring him was issued. When he died, he was buried with full honors.

Philby has been portrayed in a number of fictionalized spy stories. He is the model for Bill Haydon, the mole inside the British intelligence service, in the novel and films of *Tinker, Tailor, Soldier, Spy* by John le Carré.

Another Cambridge spy, Guy Burgess, produced programs for the BBC, and then worked for the Security Service, MI-5. Later in the war, he was recruited into a job at the Foreign Office that gave him access to secret documents. He smuggled documents out, photographed them, and then returned them. He sent the data to the Soviet Union.

After the war, he was sent to the British Embassy in Washington where he roomed with Kim Philby. Philby warned Burgess that he and fellow diplomat Donald Maclean were likely to be discovered. They escaped to Russia.

Maclean, another Cambridge spy, was a Londoner from a prominent family. He passed the civil service test and joined the Foreign Office where he held various posts. He had been recruited as a Soviet spy while at the university. He held a strong affinity with Communism and the Soviet Union. As a diplomat he rose in the ranks, and was able to inform Moscow about British and French policies and plans, British relations with Germany, and inside information in many crucial areas.

In London his Soviet contact was a woman, Kitty Harris, who passed the secrets from Maclean to Moscow. Maclean's wife, Melinda, an American, was aware that her husband was a spy.

Later, Maclean was sent to Washington where he held high posts at the British Embassy. He sat on a committee with Americans and Canadians that dealt with the atom bomb program. He passed along policy and plan information to the Soviets that proved to be priceless. He knew about the progress of the Manhattan project, timetables, and type of bombs. The Americans and British were working to discover the status of the German atomic program, information that was crucial to the Russians.

At the same time the Soviets were getting technical data on the bomb from Fuchs, May, David Greenglass, Julius, and Ethel Rosenberg. In Washington U.S. counter-intelligence agents were studying past decrypted messages sent from Moscow to Washington and New York. They picked up hints and signs of spy activities. They began to suspect two British officials, Burgess and Maclean. Philby tipped them off and they both fled to the Soviet Union.

Maclean received many honors in the Soviet Union, learned Russian and held important jobs as an adviser and policy analyst in foreign affairs.

The spy revelation that may have shocked London the most was about Anthony Blunt, Sir Anthony Blunt, cousin of the Queen Mother, confidant of the Queen, famed art historian, and keeper of the Queen's art collection. He too was recruited as a Soviet spy during his Cambridge years. He became a leading figure of the British Communist Party.

In World War II he joined the Army, and then the Security Service, MI-5. He gained access to the decoded German messages that were being deciphered by the famous code-breakers at Bletchley Park. They had broken the code generated by the German *Enigma* Machine. These efforts became the stuff of legend, and were the subject of books and movies; and marked the beginning of the computer age.

Blunt recruited an intelligence officer, John Cairncross, at Bletchley Park. Blunt was able to pass on vital intelligence about

German plans to the Soviet Union, including battle plans and troop movements.

At the end of the war he went on a secret mission to Germany to retrieve letters exchanged between Hitler and the Duke of Windsor, the former King of England, who abdicated in the 1930s and was accused of harboring pro-German sentiments—a great embarrassment to British royalty.

After the war, evidence began to point to Blunt as a spy. This was covered up for years. Finally, in 1979 Prime Minster Margaret Thatcher 'outed' Blunt as a spy in a speech in Parliament. He was stripped or honors and titles but never prosecuted.

The sheer number of Soviet-recruited spies in Britain damaged the reputation of British intelligence agencies. Some pointed out that these spies justified their activities as helping an ally defeat Hitler. They also helped the Soviets and later the Chinese obtain atomic and nuclear weapons.

The Japanese did manage to penetrate the British military by inserting a spy, an officer in the British Indian Army inside the great fortified naval port of Singapore. He fed information to the Japanese in the days leading up to the Japanese conquest of the city-state. The spy was uncovered and shot just before the fall of Singapore.

The Real James Bond

By all accounts there was a real James Bond, although the character seems to be a fusion of more than one real spy.

Commander W. 'Biffy' Dunderdale was an officer in the Secret Intelligence Service, MI-6. For a time he was in charge of the Paris office. He debriefed a top aide to Dictator Joseph Stalin. The aide had defected. In the war Dunderdale ran networks of spies and agents in occupied France.

He was described as a man of charm, savoir-faire, with a love of fast cars, and beautiful women. Of course, Ian Fleming, creator of Bond, worked at MI-6. He may have also taken inspiration from another MI-6 agent, Pieter Tazelaar, a Dutch citizen.

He was landed on the Dutch coast at the resort town of Scheveningen, near the casino. He stripped off his rubber suit and revealed a full tuxedo, complete with an odor of Hennessy XO brandy.

Despite the Cambridge spies, all was not bad news on the spying front. The British also had some notable successes, and one disastrous intelligence failure, one of the worst in history. First, the good news.

The First Space Age Target

In 1943, British and allied spy planes photographed some strange German launch sites. Were they for rockets, secret weapons, chemical and biological agents?

Then two Polish forced laborers smuggled information to the underground Polish Home Army about the German research center where they worked: Peenemunde. They passed this on to the British.

This remote facility on the Baltic Sea housed the new rocket and missile test and development facilities of the German armed forces. The site was commanded by rocket scientist, Werhner Von Braun, who would one day head the U.S. missile program that put a man on the moon.

Peenemunde was building and testing V-1 rockets, a kind of cruise missile that flew more like a plane; and the big V-2 rockets, the first-ever space rocket. These 'vengeance weapons' would have one main target: London.

In 1944, these 'secret weapons' would rain terror on the great city. Nearly 10,000 missiles and rockets would be launched at London. They would kill or wound 33,000 people and destroy or damage well over 100,000 buildings and houses. The psychological damage was devastating. V-1 missiles came in silently after the engine cut off. V-2's came down from near space with blockbuster warheads. They were not pinpoint weapons. They were terror weapons—vengeance weapons. Some Londoners left the city out of fear.

British intelligence officers fought back as best they could. For a time the raids were kept secret so the Germans would not know if they were hitting targets. They later put out false statements saying the missiles had missed their targets and blown up harmlessly in fields, even though they had hit the city. This was an attempt to trick the Germans into changing their targeting.

Then some more good news. A test V-2 rocket landed in Sweden. Neutral Sweden traded the missile to the British for Spitfire fighter planes. Another test rocket fell in Poland and was taken by the Polish underground and passed on to the British. British scientists and engineers reverse engineered the rockets and learned of their potential to destroy.

In the meantime, spy planes photographed Peenemunde and pinpointed key targets, test sites, living quarters, engineering workshops, and power plants.

The Royal Air Force then struck. It launched a night attack with 600 bombers. Some 40 planes were lost along with 215 airmen.

The order for the raid was unsparing: If the raid fails, a raid will be launched the next night and then next night, for as long as it takes.

The raid was successful. This and subsequent raids forced the Germans to disperse the rocket research and production to secure sites in Germany and Austria. The raids delayed the use of the rockets and missiles by months.

Hitler's Atom Bomb

One of the great intelligence challenges of the war was discovering Germany's progress in creating an atom bomb.

As far as knowhow and technology went, no nation was better positioned to build an atom bomb than Germany. Most of the world's atomic physicists had trained in Germany, including Robert Oppenheimer, the head of the American bomb project.

In fact, the atomic age really began in 1938 in Berlin when German chemist Otto Hahn bombarded uranium with neutrons and created a new, lighter element that resulted in a chain reaction. In other words, matter was changed into energy: $E=MC^2$, the famous Einstein equation. Hahn would win a Nobel Prize.

When this news reached the U.S. and other countries, the race to build a bomb was on. Einstein, who was living in the U.S. was persuaded to write his famous letter to President Franklin Roosevelt telling him that new research in Germany pointed to the likelihood that powerful bombs could be built. He urged the U.S. to begin a project. Soon a half dozen nations were cranking up bomb programs.

Germany did have a few liabilities. Some of the top scientists had fled the Hitler regime. Also, the decision-making process under a dictatorship was convoluted and unpredictable. A lot of power centers had to sign on to get things done. Science was heavily politicized; all Jewish scientists had left the country. Also, there needed to be sources of uranium.

Still, the great theoretical physicist Werner Heisenberg was available, along with Hahn and others. The Germans went forward with a bomb program.

In Norway, conquered by Germany, a heavy water plant was built near a waterfall in Telemark. The heavy water, deuterium oxide, would be used to 'tame' radioactivity by slowing down chain reactions in a nuclear reactor. In what was called one of the most successful sabotage operations, British forces and Norwegian resistance fighters destroyed the plant. That put a damper on the program.

The Germans decided not to put vast resources into building an atom bomb. It was put on the 'back burner'. The military, which would have had to give full support, refused to do so. Heisenberg went forward with plans to build an atomic reactor, which could be a forerunner to a bomb.

Late in the war, as Germany was falling apart, it was clear to the Americans and the British that the west should seek to evacuate top German scientists in atomic and rocket science. Their expertise would be invaluable, and they ought to be kept out of the clutches of the Soviets.

At least ten of the top atomic scientists were picked up and transported to an estate near Cambridge, England. They were held here in relative luxury for more than seven months. The British bugged the estate and listened to the conversations of Heisenberg, Otto Hahn, Kurt Diebner, and the others.

The clandestine recordings indicate the German scientists may have dragged their feet, and they were pleased they had not built an atom bomb.

Bletchley Park Code-Breakers

This story of the code-breakers is now so well known it hardly needs re-telling. After capturing a top-secret German *Enigma* code machine the decoders were able to decipher German messages and orders.

Alan Turing, who worked at the decoding center, is credited with building the first digital computer. Churchill said the decoders shortened the war and saved countless lives. Less well known is the fact the British purposefully did not pass along some decoded messages for fear of tipping off the Germans that the code had been broken.

The Soviet penetrated Bletchley Park, and two British spies, working for the Soviets, passed on decoded secret information to Moscow.

Special Operations

London spymasters and intelligence officers ran many successful spy, sabotage and clandestine operations out of a new secret agency, the Special Operations Executive.

SOE showed that the British didn't always 'play the game' in a fair fight. The agency's job was to fight dirty against an uncompromising enemy. It also gave women a chance to fight, and die and be heroes. Another chapter provides the details.

The Great Intelligence Disaster

In December 1941, the Japanese bombed the American Naval base at Pearl Harbor, and attacked the Philippines. The U.S. was at war with Japan. Hitler then declared war on the U.S.

At the same time, Japanese naval and army forces invaded Malaya, with the ultimate aim of capturing the great British naval base at Singapore, key to the straits linking the Indian and Pacific oceans.

Their strategy was to fight down the Malayan peninsula and attack Singapore island from the rear. British forces, including Indian troops and Australians, fought back.

The British sent two of their biggest and most modern warships, *The Repulse* and *Prince of Wales* to repulse the invaders at sea. Japanese planes sank both ships, with the loss of 840 sailors, including Admiral Tom Phillips. Churchill said the news of the sunken ships 'was the most shocking of the war'.

Ironically, two British aircraft carriers were delayed in catching up to the *Repulse* and *Prince of Wales*. Carrier planes might have saved the ships.

The Japanese slowly but surely pushed ahead. The British fell back until at last they had retreated to the island of Singapore, a confined territory 30 miles wide, 20 miles deep.

The British had nearly 100,000 troops, and there were 1 million civilians on the island. The huge coastal guns faced toward the sea. They could be turned, contrary to the myth that they pointed the wrong way, but the ammunition was designed to penetrate ship armor, not attack troops.

British commander General Percival felt his situation was getting more perilous. He did not have enough planes to challenge Japanese air domination. The civilian population was in a panic. The Japanese were poised to land on the island in force.

In London, Churchill sent his commanders in Singapore a chilling order: "Under no circumstances are you to surrender. Commanders and senior officers should die with their troops."

Still, the situation deteriorated. The Japanese landed 23,000 troops on the island. Percival failed to stop them, even though he had superior manpower. The Japanese pushed toward the city, threatened the water supply, and captured airfields.

General Percival met with his top officers in a concrete command bunker in the city, The Battle Box. They considered a counterattack but rejected the idea. Instead they decided to surrender, which turned out to be unconditional—a humiliating turn of events. They believed their situation was hopeless.

It was the greatest single British defeat in history. They lost 'fortress Singapore'. Some 160,000 troops were lost in the campaign, including 100,000 at Singapore. Many of these would die as prisoners forced to build a jungle railroad for the Japanese.

(This was the subject of the Academy-Award-winning film, *Bridge on the River Kwai.)*

More than anything, the defeat was a failure of intelligence and analysis of the enemy.

- The British underestimated the fighting ability of the Japanese. They dismissed them as 'little men' who could fight the Chinese but not Westerners. There was a high level of hubris, and even racism. They did not study their brutal 'no prisoners' tactics.

- The British failed to give air cover to their big warships—and they were sunk. This despite the fact the British had disabled Italian warships using torpedo planes. They didn't learn their own lesson. They did not believe the huge ships were vulnerable or that the Japanese possessed the skills to sink them.
- Most serious of all, they greatly overestimated the Japanese strength, and failed to detect that the Japanese had outrun their supplies and were running out of ammunition. The Japanese had about 30,000 troops, half the estimate of the British.

Japanese commander General Yamashita pointed to this intelligence fiasco. "My attack was a bluff. I had 30,000 men and was outnumbered three to one. I knew that if I had to fight for long for Singapore, I'd be beaten."

An Australian officer offered an assessment: "Two divisions beat us, and they were riding stolen bicycles and had no artillery."

Chapter 13
The Secret Army

Assassin Soldiers and Women Terrorists

Sixty-four Baker Street, London, was the headquarters of a secret army that would change the face of warfare. The agents, operatives and irregular soldiers controlled from here would provide fodder for dozens of books, movies, articles, and TV shows.

The British had prided themselves on 'playing the game', fighting fair in a gentlemanly fashion. Certain tactics and practices simply were not done. Outside the code. Not proper.

But this war was different. Hitler had turned his forces against civilians. Everyone was a combatant now. The Nazis had terror bombed Warsaw and Rotterdam. They had shot at civilians fleeing on the roads to create chaos and confusion. They aimed to win 'by whatever means necessary'.

Nazi Germany and Fascist Italy had invaded, conquered, or were about to conquer more than 20 nations on two continents. People in the conquered lands wanted to fight back. Churchill recognized this when he ordered a cabinet minister to create a new organization, a secret army to fight 'irregular war' that would not be constrained by the usual rules and conventions.

Thus was born the Special Operations Executive. It grew quickly to 13,000 staffers, with agents and operations all over Europe, Africa, and the Middle East. It opened dozens of training and research facilities, many in and around London.

It hired more than 3,000 women, including women who would become secret agents, infiltrators, leaders of insurgents, and resistance fighters.

What was its purpose? To create chaos, confusion, and revolt in enemy held territory. To help resistance fighters, sabotage enemy facilities and projects; assist in 'neutralizing' enemy leaders, including the use of assassination. The researchers built and invented a bewildering array of devices and techniques worthy of James Bond. Here was the forerunner to 'Q Branch' in the Bond movies.

Need explosives, a spy radio, a submarine canoe, a dead rat with a bomb inside, a roadside bomb disguised as a dung heap, a single-shot 'cigarette' pistol?

SOE provided all these things and plenty more. It also enjoyed some spectacular successes:

- It aided Czech patriots in the assassination of Reinhard Heydrich in Prague. He was the second in command of the SS.
- British commandos and Norwegian fighters raided and destroyed the heavy water plant in Telemark, Norway. This plant was an essential part of the German atom bomb project. Heavy water was needed to 'tame' runaway radiation in a chain reaction. (This inspired the Hollywood film, *Heroes of Telemark.*)
- SOE aided the Polish underground and Home Army. They in turn smuggled out the first indications of the Holocaust. Later, they provided the British with an intact German V-2 rocket.
- SOE aided resistance fighters in countless ways, air-dropped supplies and weapons, parachuted in agents and saboteurs, provided training and technical support.
- SOE developed a plan to assassinate Hitler. It was never carried out.
- It was the SOE that organized hundreds of 'suicide squads', groups of fighters who would go underground if Britain was invaded and fight the enemy from the rear. They were all expected to die in the process. For organizational purposes they were a part of the Home Guard.

SOE recruited a number of women as secret agents. Some 53 were sent into occupied Europe. A third of them died. The missions were so dangerous and critical that the agents were each given an 'L-Pill' a cyanide capsule for suicide if captured.

One of the most remarkable SOE agent stories is that of Lt. Violette Szabo. She was a French-born Londoner, who was fluent in French. She met and married an exile French soldier of the Foreign Legion. He was killed in Africa fighting for the Free French.

She in turn served in several jobs before joining an Army auxiliary, then an anti-aircraft artillery battery. She was chosen by the SOE for intensive training as a secret agent. She learned cryptography, survival tactics, use of weapons, and parachuting.

She was parachuted into France on her first mission, which she completed. She was again parachuted in. This time she and a French resistance fighter were stopped at a roadblock set up by a German armored division.

She engaged the soldiers in a gun battle with a Sten gun. She was captured, taken to Paris, interrogated, and eventually sent to a concentration camp in Germany. There she was executed.

She was given posthumous awards by Britain and France. A book about her life is called, *Young, Brave and Beautiful.* A movie was also made about her life.

Another SOE agent, Cecile Witherington, won fame with her exploits. She was parachuted into France to lead resistance fighters. She headed a network with 1,500 fighters. Those forces killed 1000 Germans and aided in the capture of 18,000.

It was SOE that generated the famous coded messages read out at the end of news broadcast from the BBC European Service, such as, '*Mon Pere a un longue moustache.*' 'My father has a long mustache.'

These messages were signals to the French underground to begin a mission. There were some famous names associated with SOE. Ian Fleming, creator of James Bond, served as a liaison officer between Naval Intelligence and the SOE. SOE's daredevil agents and eye-popping gadgetry inspired the creation of Bond and his world.

Horror film actor Christopher Lee, famed for his portrayal of Dracula and other villains, was an SOE officer. A. J. Ayer, the philosopher and promoter of 'logical positivism', was an officer in the Welsh Guards, and was assigned to SOE and later to MI-6.

A lot of the regular agencies, the military, intelligence, had a mixed opinion of SOE. They were seen as zealous amateurs playing at war and revolution. The RAF didn't want to divert planes for SOE projects.

Chapter 14
What Did You Do in the War?

Some Famous Names and Faces in Bomb-Torn London

War-time London, which was an anthill of frantic activity, interrupted by interludes of terror from the sky, was home to many famous names and faces: writers, poets, journalists, artists, spies, scientists, nation-builders, exiles, politicians, movie-makers, entertainers, and many others. Here is what was going on with notable people on a typical war-time day during the Blitz bombing.

Over at Bush House, home of the BBC's foreign broadcasts, writer *George Orwell* was writing propaganda for his radio programs aimed at India, the restless 'Jewel in the British Crown'.

Orwell was frustrated by the work, and came to believe it was futile. He called it propaganda, an effort overseen by the huge Ministry of Information housed in a London skyscraper. He was also gathering material for his future novels about the misuse and abuse of language—doublespeak sanctioned by the Ministry of Truth.

Across town poet *T. S. Eliot* was an air raid warden with a helmet, a uniform and mandate to order people to 'black out' all windows so no lights were showing—lights that would guide enemy bombers. He was an eyewitness as the bombers turned the city into a wasteland.

Writer *J. B. Priestly* delivered regular talks on the BBC Home Service, talks heard around the nation. He spoke about the war in 'people terms'. He humanized the horrible events. He warned that whatever the outcome of the war the nation would never be the same. It would have to change, to be less class-ridden, fairer to everyone, with more opportunities and better health care.

Writer and Professor *C. S. Lewis* was also giving talks on the radio. At a time when it seemed that European civilization itself was collapsing, he sought to find meaning and purpose in the death and suffering all around. He contrasted the evils of blind power and worldly ambition with the kinder and gentler vision of the Christian faith. His talks became the basis of a book, *Mere Christianity*, which still finds a large audience today.

Lewis had known war: he was a front-line soldier in World War I. His friend and fellow professor, *J. R. R. Tolkien*, famed linguist and author of *The Lord of the Rings*, was also a veteran of World War I trench warfare. He was slated to join the code-breakers at Bletchley Park, but was never called.

Novelist *Agatha Christie* was in London working at the pharmacy of the University College Hospital. Here she would learn about poisons, knowledge she would put to use as the 'Queen of Crime'. She created a stir in intelligence circles when one of her stories involving a hunt for saboteurs contained a character called Major Bletchley. Did she have inside knowledge about the code-breakers at Bletchley Park? It turns out the name was a coincidence. She would go on to become the world's best-selling novelist. Her plays and story adaptions appeared in West End theatres during the war.

Virginia Woolf, novelist and essayist, and head of her own literary circle, was directly impacted by the bombing. Her London home would be destroyed. The author of *To the Lighthouse* and *Orlando*, she had suffered from depression and what is now called bipolar disorder.

In 1941, she wrote to her husband, 'Dearest, I feel I am going mad again.' She stuffed rocks in her overcoat pockets, walked into the River Ouse and drowned. Woolf, adamantly anti-fascist, was on the SS list of Britons to be arrested after occupation.

H. G. Wells, famed writer of both history and science fiction, lived in London in the war years and died in 1946. Wells, author of *War of the Worlds*, lived to see the world at war. He had imagined new and terrible weapons; now he saw those weapons become a reality. Life imitated art.

Arthur C. Clarke, futurist and science fiction writer, and author of *2001: a Space Odyssey*, was working on the future as an operator and instructor in the new radar technology. It was radar that allowed the fighter planes to intercept the bombers before they reached their targets. Clarke was a corporal in the RAF, but rose to lieutenant. At the end of the war he would posit the possibility that earth satellites could provide worldwide radio communication. *William Golding*, author of *Lord of the Flies*, and future Nobel Prize winner, was in the thick of the fighting. He served as an officer in the Royal Navy aboard a destroyer. He participated in the pursuit and sinking of the German battleship *Bismarck*. He commanded a landing ship at the D-Day invasion of Europe, and at the Battle of Walcheren in Holland in 1944. *Lord of the Flies* is about a group of school boys, evacuated from wartime England, washed up on a deserted tropical island after a plane crashes.

Novelist *Evelyn Waugh* also saw a lot of action. He served in the Horse Guards, and later as an officer in the Royal Marines. He helped evacuate British troops from the Greek island of Crete.

In the 1939 period before hostilities began, called the Phony War, Waugh wrote a satirical novel, *Put Out More Flags*, about the absurdities of military life in peacetime.

Later in the war, when nursing injuries, he worked on his great novel, *Brideshead Revisited*, with its wartime scenes at the grand country estate turned into a military compound, where Captain Ryder confronts soldiers, such as the character Hooper, who have embraced the mundane and profane, but have lost all sense of the sacred.

Dylan Thomas, the Welsh poet, author of *Under Milk Wood*, was writing propaganda films for the Ministry of Information.

Anthony Burgess, who would go on to write the dystopian novel, *A Clockwork Orange*, spent the war in the British Army, first in the Medical Corps, then in the Army Education Corps.

An incident in London in the war prompted the writing of the novel about the government's attempt to alter the brain of a young criminal who killed a woman. Four American soldiers who had deserted from the U.S. Army robbed and raped Burgess's wife, Lynne, in her London home. She later miscarried. He was stationed in Gibraltar at the time.

Burgess was a reluctant soldier, and at one point was pursued by the Military Police for being AWOL. Even so he was promoted to sergeant and later to sergeant-major.

The great playwright *George Bernard Shaw*, too old for active service, lived part of the time at London's Fitzroy Square and the rest of the time at his country home, Shaw's Corner. Shaw, an iconoclast, Fabian socialist, and noted wit had no words to match the horrors of a world war. Several writers were drawn to spying, counter-spying and intelligence work.

Malcolm Muggeridge, journalist, editor and raconteur, worked for the Ministry of Information, but later joined the army and was sent to MI-6, the foreign intelligence service.

He was sent to Africa, with a 'cover story', and performed duties as a spy. Muggeridge was hated in Berlin and Moscow. As a journalist he covered Stalin, and was sympathetic to Communism. Later he turned against the Soviet dictator and reported on the planned famine in Russia and the Ukraine that forced the collectivization of farming.

After the war, he would edit the humor magazine, *Punch*, convert to Christianity and make known to the world a diminutive nun from Calcutta, Mother Teresa.

Ian Fleming, creator of *James Bond*, worked for Naval Intelligence, but much of his time was spent with the new secret agency, Special Operations Executive, set up to assist resistance and underground movements in Nazi-held countries.

This agency was full of real Bonds—secret agents, saboteurs, assassins with a license to kill; plus a real 'Q Branch' inventing pistols shaped like cigarettes and bombs shaped like horse dung.

Graham Greene, the novelist of cold war thrillers and serious stories with a Catholic world view, worked at MI-6 as an intelligence operative. His boss was Kim Philby, who was a Soviet agent who had penetrated the core of British intelligence and diplomacy.

Later Greene's books would be made into a whole succession of movies: *The Third Man, the Quiet American, the Comedians, Our Man in Havana, the Fallen Idol, The Power and the Glory.*

Somerset Maugham, already world famous as a novelist in 1940, and a former intelligence officer, had to flee from the

Germans from his home on the French Riviera. Maugham spent much of the war in the U.S. where he made pro-British speeches. He returned to London in 1944.

Traitor?

P. G. Wodehouse, the humorist and novelist, also fled the Nazis—but he didn't make it. He was captured in France and sent to Germany. He was persuaded or coerced into making several broadcasts to Britain on German radio. These 'talks' were light and not political or anti-British but they enraged the British public. Some suggested the broadcasts were treasonous.

Wodehouse, who seemed to have captured the essence of the English upper class, with Bertie Wooster and his butler, Jeeves, was more naïve than sinister.

Late in the war he met in Paris with British journalists. Any talk of a treason charge was dropped, but Wodehouse moved to the United States after the war.

The Journalists

Edward R. Murrow, American journalist and radio reporter reported on the bombing of London live and direct in a series of dramatic broadcasts for CBS Network.

"This is London…" Murrow would begin his broadcasts. They would make him famous and he would go on to become a major television news presence in the U.S.

William Shirer, another American and radio colleague of Murrow. Shirer was in Berlin and reported the British bombing raids on the German capital in 1940. Shirer's reports were heavily censored, and by late 1940, he was afraid the Gestapo would charge him, falsely, with espionage. He got out. He went on to write books about the war period.

Walter Cronkite was a reporter in Europe and flew as a journalist on bombing runs over Germany conducted by the American 8th Air Force. Cronkite would go on to become the famous anchor of the nightly television news program for CBS.

Andy Rooney, who would win fame for his personal commentaries on the American TV news magazine, *60 Minutes*, was a reporter in London for the American forces newspaper, *Stars and Stripes*.

David Low, political cartoonist for *the London Evening Standard*, a national newspaper, skewered the dictators, Hitler, Stalin, and Mussolini to the point where his cartoons prompted complaints from the governments. They prompted a warning from Germany. Low was put on the SS's list of those to be arrested when Britain was occupied.

Actors and Filmmakers

Actors, actresses and filmmakers joined the war effort. Some served in the military and were given leave to act on stage and in films.

The film industry, centered on London and its suburbs, switched to making propaganda films, patriotic tales, and documentaries. Some of them are considered classics of the cinema.

Noel Coward, playwright, actor, and film director, made movies, wrote plays and acted in West End productions. He was also an officer in the Royal Navy. His war film, *In Which We Serve*, won great praise. At the same time his play, *Blithe Spirit*, was performed 2,000 times at the Savoy Theater.

Laurence Olivier followed a similar track. He was a Hollywood film star when war broke out. He and his wife, Vivien Leigh, who had starred in *Gone with the Wind*, returned to London. He was a pilot and was assigned to the Navy's Fleet Air Arm. He was also given leave to act on stage and in films. Winston Churchill himself encouraged Olivier to direct and star in a big color film of Shakespeare's *Henry V*, an epic of war and knights in shining armor. The film won much critical acclaim, plus two Academy Awards.

London-born actor *Alec Guinness*, who would star in countless films, and win his greatest fame in *Star Wars*, served in combat in the Royal Navy commanding a landing craft in Sicily. He also ferried military supplies to partisan fighters in Yugoslavia.

Actor *David Niven* also had a Hollywood career, and had leading roles with Errol Flynn, Ginger Rogers. Still, he elected to return to England. He was an army veteran and was recommissioned as a lieutenant and sent to a commando special forces unit known as 'The Phantom'. He saw action in Europe, at Normandy. He rose to the rank of Lt. Colonel.

Churchill himself singled out Niven: "You did a fine thing to give up your film career to serve your country."

Niven also worked on films for the Army Film Unit. He made a much-praised film about the British Army fighting Rommel's Afrika Korps in North Africa, *The Way Ahead*.

One of his fellow actors, *Peter Ustinov*, a mere private, was made an aide to Niven. Ustinov, actor, director, and playwright, would go on to win two Academy Awards for best supporting actor.

Comedian *Peter Sellers*, who would go on to lasting fame in *Dr. Strangelove* and as Inspector Clouseau in the *Pink Panther films*, served in the war in the Royal Air Force. He was just 18, but managed to get a performance spot with a troupe, The Gang Show, that performed for the soldiers. The troupe toured India, Burma, and Ceylon. Sellers was also a first-rate drummer.

Actor *Herbert Lom* was working at the BBC's German language service at Bush House in Central London. He would go on to play Commissioner Dreyfus, the frantic boss of Sellers' Inspector Clouseau in the *Pink Panther*.

Actor *Christopher Lee*, movie villain, Dracula, a James Bond nemesis, Scaramanga, and many more in the Hammer Film horror movies, worked at the secret spy and sabotage agency, SOE.

A number of film directors were working on films across London, including propaganda films: *David Lean, Anthony Asquith, Powell and Pressburger, Carol Reed, Val Guest, Robert Hamer,* and *Alberto Cavalcanti*. In the post-war years they would create a kind of Golden Age for British cinema, an age that ended in the late 1950s with the rise of television.

One young Londoner, Michael Micklewhite, eight-year-old son of Cockney working-class parents, was one of those sent out of London for safety. He went to a small town in the County of Norfolk to sit out the Blitz.

After the war, he studied acting and changed his name to Michael Caine. He would go on to become a movie star in Britain and America. He'd win several Academy Awards and appear in 115 movies.

The Musicians

William Walton, composer of music for Royal Coronations, including the march *Crown Imperial*, wrote music for the movies, including Olivier's epic, *Henry V*. His London home was destroyed by the bombing. Composer *Benjamin Britten* was given the rare status of conscientious objector. He worked on his opera, *Peter Grimes.*

Igor Stravinsky, famed composer, spent the war years in the U.S. In 1945, he came to London for the performance of his *Firebird Suite.* Ralph Vaughn Williams, composer, was a combat veteran of World War I. Now in his seventies, he continued to compose and conduct during the war. In 1943, he conducted his own music at the Proms concerts, including his *Symphony #5.*

London's orchestras played under the batons of leading conductors: *John Barbirolli, Malcolm Sargent, Adrian Boult.*

In the Long Run We're Dead

All over the city men and women were preparing to fight a war. Over at the Bank of England, economist *John Maynard Keynes* was trying to figure out how to pay for the war.

Keynes became famous for his theories of deficit financing, with tax money and debt used to stimulate the economy in hard times, with the debt paid off in good times. This became 'Keynesian economics'. His theories would influence governments around the world and provoke much controversy.

Now as a director of the Bank of England he knew that piling debt on top of debt was the only way to pay in the short run. It was Keynes who had said, "In the long run we are all dead."

As the bombs fell those words came into sharp focus. Late in the war he developed new ideas for a world financial system, including a single world-wide currency. He was successful with his own finances, became a millionaire, an art collector, and was close friends with the Bloomsbury literary circle that included Virginia Woolf and T. S. Eliot.

The Handsome Fascist

London-born politician *Oswald Mosley* seemed to have everything. He was strikingly handsome. He was smart, well-educated; he married well. He had been in the government and in Parliament. Politically, he was all over the map: conservative, then on the left.

He became fascinated with Italian dictator Benito Mussolini and his Fascist Party. In 1931, Mosley created the British Union of Fascists, which claimed a membership of 50,000.

He imitated many of the trappings and policies of Fascism and Nazi-ism on the Continent. In 1936, his followers marched through a heavily Jewish district of East London. They were met with resistance from the local people in what became known as the 'Battle of Cable Street'.

As Hitler rose to power and began to threaten his neighbors, Mosley saw his stock plummet. When war broke out, he was arrested as a security threat, and was confined, along with his wife, on the grounds of London's Holloway Prison, in a detached house.

Later in the war he was released but kept under house arrest. After the war, he went back to civilian life and lived another 35 years.

Life vs. Death

Thousands were dying in what was becoming a world war. Millions would die in the coming four years. Over at London's St. Mary's Hospital a medical researcher was perfecting a treatment that would save millions of lives.

Alexander Fleming had discovered a mold on bread that could kill deadly bacteria. He called it penicillin, the first in the class of antibiotics.

He would be awarded the Nobel Prize for medicine. Researchers at Oxford University would develop methods of mass producing penicillin. By the end of the war penicillin was widely available to fight off killer infections.

Across the city at the Admiralty Research Laboratory a young researcher was figuring out how to build better explosive mines for use in the Navy. His lab was damaged by bombs. *Francis Crick* would switch from physics and mines to cellular studies at Cambridge University. He would go on to be the co-discoverer of the DNA molecule, which would win him a Nobel Prize.

Other top scientists were working on means of mass killing. *Paul Dirac*, who won the Nobel Prize at age 31, and who held the prestigious title of *Lucasian Professor of Mathematics* at Cambridge University, the chair held by Isaac Newton, was working on ways to enrich uranium to make atomic bombs using centrifuges. It's a technique still in use today.

The famously quirky and taciturn Dirac once traveled with top German atomic physicist Werner Heisenberg. Dirac, at a loss for words, finally said to Heisenberg, "I have a new equation. Have you got one?"

Birth of the Paralympics

Early in 1939 German neurologist *Dr. Ludwig Guttmann* and his whole family left Germany for Britain. He was a prominent researcher into spinal injuries, but he was also Jewish and could see nothing but a bleak future if he stayed.

At Oxford he received help from refugee aid groups. In 1943, with the war raging, British officials asked Guttmann to form a special spinal injury program for the war wounded. He was installed at a hospital in Buckinghamshire just outside London where he ran the new National Spinal Injury Clinic.

He developed a theory that sports could help those with spinal cord injuries. Sports assisted them physically and mentally by giving them feelings of accomplishment and self-worth in the face of crippling injuries.

The injured began playing games in wheelchairs and in the swimming pool. This expanded into the Paraplegic Games held in the town of Stoke-Mandeville and at the hospital. More teams and games were added, and teams came from other countries.

After the war, the games grew even more, and were renamed the Paralympics, a movement that eventually went world-wide. They were tied in with the Olympics, and garnered support from governments and the private sector.

Dr. Guttmann was knighted by Queen Elizabeth II.

The Killer Theologian

Robert Runcie, a student at Oxford, joined the army and served in the Scots Guards. He became a tank commander and served in a number of fights in WWII. In one engagement he saved a fellow soldier. In another fight his tank destroyed three enemy anti-tank guns. He won a combat medal. His unit helped liberate the Bergen-Belsen Concentration Camp.

After the war, Runcie resumed studies at Oxford and at Cambridge. He received a degree in theology and was ordained a priest in the Church of England.

In 1979, after serving in several high church jobs, he was named Archbishop of Canterbury, the top post in the Church of England and the worldwide Anglican communion.

He would perform the marriage ceremony of Princess Diana and Prince Charles. He would welcome Pope John Paul VI to England.

Runcie was the only Archbishop of Canterbury ever to have killed enemy soldiers in battle.

A Young Lieutenant from Windsor

Princess Elizabeth, the future Queen of England, was just 13 when the war broke out in 1939.

She and her younger sister, Margaret, spent most of the war at Windsor Castle near London. It was the largest inhabited castle in the world.

Government officials suggested that the princesses be sent to Canada for safety. The King and Queen rejected the idea. The Queen said, "The children won't go without me. I won't leave without the King. And the King will never leave."

The fact that the Royal Family stayed in London did a lot to endear them to the people. They were willing to face the Blitz with everyone else. Buckingham palace was bombed. The King and Queen toured the bombed-out neighborhoods.

At 14, Princess Elizabeth spoke on a BBC children's program. Many children had been evacuated from the cities. She said, "We are trying to bear our share of the danger and sadness of war."

In 1945, as victory neared, she joined the army, the women's Auxiliary Territorial Service, and trained as a mechanic and truck driver. The future queen changed oil and checked spark plugs. She attained the rank of lieutenant—Lt. Elizabeth Windsor of Windsor. She later rose to captain.

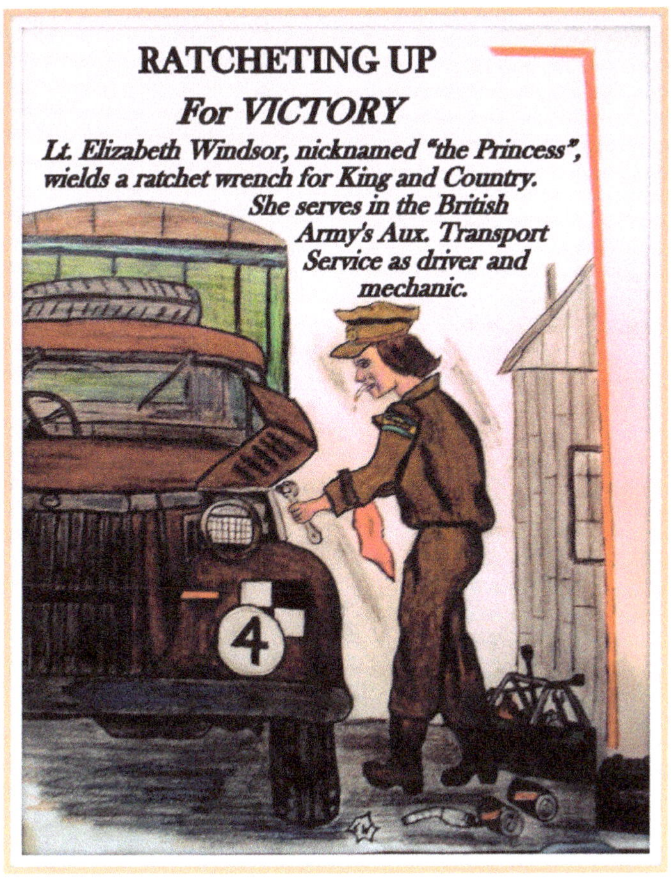

When the war in Europe did end, she and her sister anonymously took to the London streets and mingled with the happy throng. It might have been one of the few times in her life when she could act like an ordinary person.

She had served her country in uniform, as did millions. It would be a badge of honor, and another reason why people think highly of their Queen. She would serve as queen longer than any other monarch, including Queen Victoria.

No new age would be named for her, no equivalent of Victorian or Elizabethan. She would come of age in the war, a war that would mark the beginning of the end of the Empire.

Within a couple of years India would gain independence, the new nation of Pakistan would be spun off from India. By the 1960s, most colonies, protectorates, and dependencies would be gone. The sun would set. Britain would settle into a new role as a regional power in the European Union, and with a one-sided 'special relationship' with the U.S.

Germany would emerge as the economic and even political leader of Europe and the EU.

Chapter 15
The Black Book

Hitler's List of Britons to be Arrested after a Successful Invasion

The SS Security Service, as part of its plan to occupy Britain, drew up a list of prominent people to be arrested and probably eliminated.

The list included political leaders, writers, journalists, intellectuals, exiles, and refugees, and those deemed 'anti-Nazi'.

The list, published as a book, contained 2,830 names. Some 20,000 copies were published, but most were destroyed when a warehouse was bombed. Only three copies remain.

Politicians:

Winston S. Churchill, Prime Minister, former head of the Navy, former minister of colonies, former Home Secretary, and veteran military officer.

Clement Atlee, Deputy Prime Minister, head of the Labour Party—Socialist.

Anthony Eden, Foreign Secretary, member of the War cabinet. His son, a navigator in the Royal Air Force, disappeared in Burma.

Neville Chamberlain, former Prime Minister, he tried to appease Hitler, then declared war on Germany after the invasion of Poland.

Duff Cooper, Minister of Information, he was particularly against any appeasement of Hitler; he served in a number of high government posts, and was ambassador to France at the end of the war.

Stafford Cripps, leading Labour party leader, he was a staunch socialist and devoted Christian; he had a close wartime relationship with the Soviet Union, and served as ambassador. He helped negotiate independence for India.

Lord Beaverbrook, newspaper magnate, he served as minister of air craft production in the war cabinet.

Beatrice Webb, political organizer and theorist, she helped found the Labor party through her Fabian Society. She and her husband, Sidney Webb, founded the London School of Economics.

Robert Lord Vansittart of Denham, Britain's top diplomat for a number of years, and head of the Diplomatic Service. He was anti-Hitler and anti-German from the beginning of Hitler's rise and a fierce opponent of appeasement. He wrote a book, *The Black Record*, which portrayed Germany as an aggressor through the ages. He also wrote plays, novels, poetry, and worked in the film industry with his friend Alexander Korda, head of Denham Studios/ London Films. Vansittart's title included the name of the town where the film studio was located, Denham.

Foreign Leaders in exile:

General Charles de Gaulle, leader of the Free French.

Edward Benes, President of Czechoslovakia.

Jan Masaryk, foreign minister of Czechoslovakia.

Ignacy Jan Paderewski, concert pianist, composer, former foreign minister of Poland. He would die on a visit to the United States during the war. His coffin remained inside the Maine Memorial at Arlington National Cemetery in Virginia until the fall of Communism in Poland. His body was then returned to Poland with great ceremony.

Cultural and social figures:

Chaim Weizmann, British scientist, who was head of the World Zionist Organization. He would become first president of the new State of Israel.

Sigmund Freud, famed psychoanalyst and Jewish refugee from Vienna. (He was on the list even though he was deceased.)

Robert Baden-Powell, founder of the Boy Scouts. The Nazis were suspicious of the Scouts, and believed they were a recruiting ground for British military.

Noel Coward, playwright, actor, filmmaker, he was a homosexual.

Virginia Woolf, novelist, leader of a London literary circle. She committed suicide in 1941.

Alexander Korda, film producer, owner of a movie studio, he was a refugee from Hungary.

J. B. Priestly, writer, playwright, he gave social commentary on the BBC.

Bertrand Russell, prominent philosopher and mathematician.

Vic Oliver, actor, comic, he was from Vienna and was Jewish. He became a radio star and a leading entertainer in Britain. He married Sarah Churchill, the Prime Minister's daughter.

Sarah Churchill, actress, Churchill's daughter.

David Low, political cartoonist, and arch foe of Hitler, Stalin, and Mussolini.

H. G. Wells, historian, writer of science fiction.

Stefan Zweig, famed novelist from Vienna, he fled to Britain after the rise of Hitler. He was Jewish and as the threat of an invasion of Britain increased he left for the United States.

Rebecca West, London-born novelist, was a staunch anti-fascist who attacked any effort to appease Hitler.

Sylvia Pankhurst, suffragette leader. She was a strong opponent of fascism, particularly after Mussolini attacked Ethiopia. She became an advisor to Ethiopian Emperor Haile Salassie. When she died she was given a state funeral in Addis Ababa.

Paul Robeson, American actor and all-American football player, he made movies in Britain and played *Othello* at London's *Savoy Theater*. He went to the Soviet Union and praised the Soviet and Communist system. Back in London he studied African history and culture, and fought against the rise of fascism. By the time the Black Book was published he had returned to the U.S.

Nancy Astor, Lady Astor, American-born socialite and long-time Member of Parliament. She was accused of harboring pro-German sentiments, and of meeting with 'appeasers' of Hitler at her grand estate, Cliveden. She later turned against the appeasers and voted against Chamberlain in Parliament.

She had a strained relationship with Winston Churchill. In one legendary exchange, she said to Churchill, "If you were my husband, I'd put poison in your tea."

He replied, "Madame, if I was your husband, I'd drink it."

Chapter 16
Up from Ruins

It's said that Britain won a war, lost an empire, and then went searching for a role in the world. The same could be said for London.

After brief celebrations, the city was jerked back to reality: thousands of ruined buildings and houses, wrecked infrastructure, enormous debts, private companies bankrupt from the war, and a continuing need for rationing and austerity.

In Europe, a new menace arose: Communist control over Eastern Europe, hostility toward the West and the descent of what Churchill called 'An Iron Curtain'.

Overseas, the Empire grew restless. India pushed now for full independence; it had supported Britain in the war, and the British Indian Army enrolled two million volunteer soldiers. They fought the Japanese, and in Africa, and the Middle East.

Now the independence leaders, Gandhi, Nehru, and the Moslem leader Jinnah, wanted the British to 'quit India'.

In Palestine, militant Jewish groups were turning to violence against the British forces to press for action on a new State of Israel. The region's Arabs were ready to fight to stop a new nation in their midst. The stage was set for conflict that would last into the next century.

Other British possessions were restless and ready to fight to gain freedom. That was true in Malaya and parts of Africa.

Over the next quarter century the sun would begin to set on the Empire. It was a process that seemed to confirm lines in Queen Victoria's favorite hymn, *The Day Thou Gavest Lord is Ended*, which is often played at military sunset ceremonies: 'Earth's proud empires pass away.'

All that's left today are a few islands scattered in the world's oceans. Bermuda, the British Virgin Islands, Falkland Islands, and others.

The substitute for the Empire became the Commonwealth of Nations, which was held together voluntarily based on historical, cultural, and commercial ties. The British monarch remains a figurehead symbol of this loose alliance of a score of nations, from Canada to India.

The United States emerged from the war as a super-power. Its cities had not been bombed, its industries, and infrastructure remained intact. Its economy took off, fueled by pent-up demand and the return of millions of soldiers eager to build families, go to college, and start businesses and careers.

Militarily the United States dominated, with the strongest army, navy, air force, plus a nuclear arsenal and new rockets that could strike anywhere on the planet.

For Europe, including Britain everything seemed to be in decline. The Continent was divided into two hostile camps, East and West; Communist and Free. For Germany the country had to start all over again. A film about those years is titled: *Germany: Year Zero*.

A new conflict arose, the Cold War that sometimes broke into hot clashes. Now both sides had nuclear weapons and rockets. Philosophically, the mood was grim. Absurdist plays and an existential world-view took hold. The world was pointless, meaningless, absurd, and individuals had to decide for themselves how they would live their lives. All institutions were broken and suspect. Writers Sartre, Camus, Beckett, and Ionesco set the tone with books and plays that preached hopelessness.

In Britain those years, 1946 into the early and mid-1950s, are remembered for their austerity, the air of shabbiness, the shortages and rationing, and the drive to export goods to pay for all the imports of food, oil, and raw products.

London was still filled with ruined buildings or empty lots where bombed-out buildings stood. The city declined. People immigrated to Canada and Australia. A series of New Towns purposefully built siphoned off people. The vital railways, which had been devastated by war, and then nationalized, needed restructuring—rationalizing. Downsizing. That was true of many industries now in the government's hands. The term 'redundancy' came into wide use. It stood for jobs being eliminated. This caused great turmoil with the powerful labor unions.

After a study, a civil servant, Dr. Richard Beeching, closed thousands of railway stations across the country. Countless little towns and villages lost service, sending them into decline. The 'axe' eliminated 6,000 miles of rail lines.

The closings, redundancies, and immigration became signs of decline. London was now the grandiose but slightly shabby capital of a nation past its prime and headed for a slow and steady downhill course.

A New Europe

On the Continent there were signs of renewal. A new political movement took hold led by a new group of leaders. In Germany Konrad Adenauer, former mayor of Cologne and an anti-Nazi, helped form a new political party, the Christian Democratic Union. Similar parties sprang up in Austria, Italy, Belgium, and Holland. The aim was to find a 'third way' that avoided the deadly extremes of Communism and Marxism on the one side, Fascism and Nazi-ism on the other. The third way would look forward to democracy, and back to Europe's Christian roots.

Adenauer, Jean Monnet of France, Robert Schuman, Alcide de Gasperi of Italy and others joined together to write the Treaty of Rome that would create organizations that became the European Union, largely eliminating the threat of wars in a region that had battled for a thousand years.

Britain did not join in at this point. London now was the capital of a middle-sized European nation, outside the Continental union, and with a decidedly unequal 'special relationship' with the U.S.

Germany—West Germany—experienced an 'economic miracle' of growth and prosperity with increased political influence. Britons wondered, 'Who won the war?' Britain did join the defense alliance, the North Atlantic Treaty Organization that agreed to a joint military response to any Soviet encroachment on the West. Britain also pursued its own atomic and nuclear program, which developed atomic and nuclear bombs, and nuclear power reactors. The country joined the nuclear club of the U.S., Russia, and France. China, pushing to catch up, would be helped by the British nuclear spy, Klaus Fuchs.

London also played a role on a worldwide stage in this post-war period. On January 10, 1946 the General Assembly of the United Nations held its first meeting at London's Westminster Central Methodist Hall near the Parliament. Some 51 nations were present. Presiding as acting secretary general was Gladwyn Jebb, British civil servant in the Foreign Office. A week later the Security Council met for the first time, and decided to favor the peaceful use of the atom.

In the economy Britain ran a large trade deficit. It imported far more than it sold abroad. Although it produced large amounts of coal, oil and much energy had to be imported. Meat, fresh fruit, and even timber had to be shipped in from overseas. The people had to work hard and long, export and produce or die. Labor unions were accused by management of fostering strikes and work slow-downs. Class warfare and unrest grew.

J. B. Priestley had said in the war that nothing would be the same. He was proving to be right.

Look Back in Anger

Films, novels, and plays reflected the spirit of decline and decay. A whole series of movies was released featuring working class folks, often young men, beaten down or defeated by 'the system', hide-bound businesses, class distinctions that condemned people for the way they spoke or for their habits and lifestyles.

John Osborne, London-born playwright, captured the dark mood of the 1950s in his ground-breaking play, *Look Back in Anger*, which opened at the Royal Court Theater in 1956. The lead character, Jimmy Porter, was the original 'angry young man', ranting and raving against society, unfairness, hypocrisy, and the ordinariness of everyday life.

"Let's have a game where we are actually human beings and pretend to be alive," he cried. Porter was the first of a series of angry young men. This was the 'New Wave', or 'social realism', as it became known, and included writers such as Alan Sillitoe, Brendan Behan, and filmmakers Tony Richardson, Lindsay Anderson, and John Schlesinger. They produced 'angry' stories

and films, *The Borstal Boy, Loneliness of the Long Distance Runner, Billy Liar,* and *Saturday.*
Night and Sunday Morning.

In Osborne's *The Entertainer*, the aging vaudevillian Archie Rice produces and performs in a song-and-dance revue at a half-empty theater in a down-at-heels seaside resort town. The jokes seemed old, the songs out-of-date, and all around the world seemed to be coming unglued. Was this a metaphor for post-war Britain? Many saw it that way.

Glimmers

All was not gloom. There were some bright spots, glimmers of renewal. British technology produced the first commercial jet airliner, the Comet, which would revolutionize air travel. The Hovercraft, which rode the water on a cushion of air, was another technological innovation.

In the 1960s, huge oil and gas deposits were found beneath the North Sea spread over an area the size of Texas. In coming years this energy source would produce trillions of dollars' worth of wealth, money that otherwise would have been spent on imports.

Britain joined the European Union and participated in most of the programs for agriculture, development, trade, and culture fostered by the common market. It did not join the single currency, the Euro.

As prosperity returned and austerity faded, London was transformed with new construction. A whole new economic and office district, Canary Wharf, was built in the old East End Docklands. The financial and banking center, the City, thrived as a general prosperity returned.

London became a hotspot of pop culture, youth culture, and fashion. This was the new 'swinging London' of Carnaby Street, the Beatles, Twiggy, super-slender models, garish fashions, the cool, the trendy in art, publishing, and films.

This was 'Cool Britannia', which was exported to the world—music, excellent television programming, films, plays, clothes, and the examples of universal health care and the welfare state. *Monty Python* humor, and the darker vision of *A Clockwork Orange*.

The Angry Young Man gave way to the slender young trend-setter in the mini-skirt. Swinging London didn't last but it was fun for a time, and was in sharp contrast to the war and early post-war years.

The World Comes to London

Great cities renew themselves. London lost its empire, but then a portion of that empire came to London.

At the end of World War II London was a remarkably homogeneous city. The vast majority of the population originated in the British Isles—English, Scots, Welsh, and the Northern Irish. There were some people from the Irish Republic. There was a Chinatown. English was the universal language. Christianity was the near-universal religion, with a sizeable Jewish community. The Monarch served as Defender of the Faith and head of the Church of England.

The people had been stoical in the war, had endured much, in what became known as 'the people's war'. There were celebrations, prayers were offered by the King and Queen, and for the King and Queen at St. Paul's and Westminster Abbey. Then people went back to work.

"We saved ourselves by our own exertions," said Lord Woolton, Minister of Reconstruction and former Minister of Food. He noted that Marshal Göring had sworn to 'rub out London'.

London was not cowed or destroyed—'London, thou pride of cities, all.'

London remained, but it was destined to change. After the war, new immigration rules made it easier for people to come into the country from the old Empire and the new Commonwealth. This would change the city profoundly. For instance, in 1950 there were 15,000 West Indians, particularly Jamaicans, in London. By 1961 there were 172,000 and in 2011 some 600,000.

A small West Indian festival begun in 1959 that grew into the Notting Hill West Indian Festival, the largest street festival in Europe, with 1.5 million participants.

A similar story occurred for immigrants from India, Pakistan, Bangladesh, Nigeria, Kenya, and the Middle East. By 2011, the census showed the city-shaking changes. Now only

45% of the population were 'British'. Christians accounted for just 50% of the population. Now 43% were non-white. Asians were 18% of the population and blacks 13%. 37% were foreign born, led by Poles, Indians, Nigerians; 22% spoke a language other than English.

There were more than one million Moslems, compared to around four million Christians. The Hindu population was quite large.

Here was the breakdown:

- Asians: 1.5 million, led by 550,000 Indians. There were 130,000 Chinese.
- Blacks: 1.1 million, including West Indians, and Africans.
- Mixed race: 400,000.
- Non-British whites: 1 million, from Europe, the Americas, Mediterranean.

The changes altered the city in countless ways. Like Indian food? There were now plenty of Indian restaurants to choose from. You could now hear Reggae music in the streets, and African rhythms; and see the clothes and costumes of scores of lands. The burka, the flowing robe, and the turban became regular sights.

Mosques multiplied to accommodate the large Moslem population. Some harbored militant and hard-core Moslem fundamentalists. Some embraced violence. London became a media hub for Arabic language publications and broadcasting.

Rich foreigners also discovered London. It became a haven for Russian oligarchs and Saudi princes, plus the nervous rich from around the world in search of a safe home away from home.

Someone commented, "London is a paradise for the ultra-rich." Many bought or leased luxury London apartments or homes that stand empty most of the time.

Those flocking to London from troubled parts of the world found stability, money, the good life, and freedom. Some came for medical care.

New high-rise towers and skyscrapers arose, including the 1,000-foot Shard; plus architecturally standout places such as

Lloyds of London headquarters, and the Millennium Dome. The London Eye, the giant Ferris wheel, became a tourist fixture.

The city prospered. In 1940, there were 3 million motor vehicles in the entire country. Now there were nearly that many in London alone. Still, nearly half the population had no cars, and relied on the subway, the Underground that carried more than 3 million passengers a day.

For the less-than-affluent, life in London got harder and less affordable. It was always on the list of the world's most expensive cities. According to one survey reported by Forbes, London was the 12th most expensive city in 2014 out of 211 in the report.

The average house price in London hit $750,000 in 2014. Heathrow Airport became the world's busiest for international travel, with 73 million passengers a year. Five other airports serve the greater area.

In 2015, the city's population reached nearly 8.7 million, the most ever, and more than the previous peak of 8.6 million in 1940.

Those days of 1940 and 1941 when the metropolis burned are memories now, marked in blue plaques, and memorials and a statue here and there; a chapel with chiseled names of the dead. For all the changes some things have not changed. The grandeur of the great buildings; the curve of Fleet Street; the flashing signs of Piccadilly Circus; red Double-decker buses and black cabs; and the welcoming Rondel sign of the Underground.

There's misty and rainy days and nights; the wonder of clean marble and old tombs; church bells that say, *Oranges and Lemons*. Snatches of old poems, '*there's much to be seen before we go to Paradise by way of Kensal Green*'.

As in the past there's still dark-wood pubs with not-bad grub and pints of real ale; and the real English breakfast in a nice old hotel, with tea and cakes at four. Unchanged too are the clatter of Household Cavalry, the march of grenadiers in great hats; the ceremonies and choirs of monarchy; the skirl of bag pipes of the Scots or Irish Guards.

London endures and thrives. But it may be said of the city at war what Churchill said of those pilots guarding the city: "This was the finest hour."

London tries to remember the war years. A number of memorials have been erected around the city. Among the best known: War Memorials built to remember the Australians and New Zealanders. These are at Hyde Park Corner.

There is a Canadian memorial in Green Park, with the inscription, 'In two world wars, one million Canadians came to Britain and joined the fight for freedom.'

A memorial remembers the airmen and soldiers from Poland. A memorial in the City honors the 'London Troops', the soldiers who served in various London-recruited regiments.

The Merchant Navy is remembered with its memorial to those of the merchant ships and the fishing fleets, 'who gave their lives for their country and have no grave but the sea.'

One of the newest memorials is the Monument to the Women of World War II in Whitehall near the Cenotaph. It was dedicated in 2005 by the Baroness Boothroyd, the former Speaker of the House of Commons.

When looking back to the war years, and forward to today, the words of the old patriotic song ring true:

Still more majestic shalt thy rise,
More dreadful from each foreign stroke;
As the loud blast that tears the skies
Serves but to root thy native oak.

BRITISH TROOPS MARCH WITH THEIR FRENCH ALLIES

Appendix
Military and Civil Defense Forces Commanded from London; Losses in the City WWII

****Armed Forces and Civil Defense (Peak Strength)**

Commanders: Chief of the Imperial Staff:
Field Marshall *Sir Alan Brooke;*
First Sea Lord: *Admiral Sir Dudley Pound*
Chief of the Air Staff: Air Marshal *C.F.A. Portal.*
British Army: 3.5 million.
Royal Air Force: 1.2 million.
Royal Navy: 873,000.
Including: 78,000 Royal Marines.
80,000 RAF Regiment ground force.
480,000 women in three branches.
Plus—300,000 Canadians serving in Britain.

- Thousands of Australians and New Zealanders, including 13,000 Aussies in the RAF.
- Polish Corps, Jewish Brigade, etc. 100,000+ Home Guard—Special Local Defense Force: 1.6 million. British Indian Army—served in India, Middle East, Africa, Burma, Malaya: 2.0 million.

Civil Defense—Fire, Rescue, Air Raid Precaution, Police, Nursing, Ambulance Corps: 2 million.
Includes London Metropolitan Police: 44,000

TOTAL: 11,573,000

LOSSES IN LONDON from aerial bombing, rocket, missile attacks:

- Houses and buildings damaged or destroyed: 1.5 million.
- Killed 32,000 Wounded 85,000.
- Evacuated or voluntarily left the city: Blitz: 2 million, including children sent to the countryside, small towns.
- Evacuated or left the city: Rocket attacks: 1.5 million, including children sent out on the 'doodlebug expresses'—special trains.

The war left London with an acute housing shortage, which would not be remedied for years. On the practical side the bombing did clear East End slums, which were replaced by drab blocks of flats.

The city's great museums and galleries were empty as priceless art and artifacts were removed for safekeeping. The galleries were empty for years. Much of the art would have been destroyed or damaged in the bombing.

The subway, the Underground, saw lines and stations close for use as bomb shelters, storage for artworks, and even for the installation of an airplane factory.

Revival: in 1940 London counted a population of 8.6 million, its largest to that time, and for many years to come. In the years after the war the population fell below 7 million as many people relocated to a series of New Towns ringing the city.

Today—2018—the city's population is pushing toward 9 million, its greatest ever. An estimated 13 million live in the commuting zone.

Gallery

The author, an illustrator, has created more than a dozen original color illustrations of the war years with London themes: Blitz over London; Bush House, home of BBC radio 'propaganda' World Service; Churchill views, night Blitz from atop Treasury Building; the Dunkirk 'little ships'; a 'dummy city' acts as decoy against German bombers; a train and engine are wrecked by the aerial bombardment; crowds and buses flow through Piccadilly Circus; soldiers board a train at a London train station; West End theaters are lit up at night; St. Paul's Dome viewed through smoke and fire as the Fire Brigade and Rescue personnel battle the flames; British troops and bands march in the Bastille Day Parade in Paris just prior to the start of World War II, etc.

CPSIA information can be obtained
at www.ICGtesting.com
Printed in the USA
LVHW070505140619
621214LV00024B/242/P

9 781641 821445